W9-DEW-931

PENGUIN BOOKS

BY LAND, BY AIR, BY SEA

Steve and Ruth Bennett are the authors of numerous activity books designed to give busy parents a jump-start on creative play. In addition to *Cabin Fever: 202 Activities for Turning Rainy Days, Snow Days, and Sick Days into Great Days,* the couple are also the authors of the best-selling *365 TV-Free Activities You Can Do with Your Child* and *365 Outdoor Activities You Can Do with Your Child.*

They also wrote *Kick the TV Habit!,* which offers a complete program for changing your family's television-watching habits and contains one hundred TV-free activities.

Steve has written more than fifty books on parenting, the environment, business management, and microcomputing. The former president of a technical publishing company, he holds a master's degree in Regional Studies from Harvard.

Ruth is an illustrator and landscape architect who has designed public parks and playgrounds in a number of cities in the United States. She holds a master's degree in landscape architecture from the University of Virginia.

The Bennetts live with their two children, Noah and Audrey, in Cambridge, Massachusetts. And, yes, they do a lot of traveling together.

Steve and Ruth Bennett

BY LAND,

BY AIR

BY SEA

The Ultimate
Family Travel Activity Book

PENGUIN BOOKS

PENGUIN BOOKS
Published by the Penguin Group
Penguin Books USA Inc., 375 Hudson Street,
New York, New York 10014, U.S.A.
Penguin Books Ltd, 27 Wrights Lane, London W8 5TZ, England
Penguin Books Australia Ltd, Ringwood, Victoria, Australia
Penguin Books Canada Ltd, 10 Alcorn Avenue,
Toronto, Ontario, Canada M4V 3B2
Penguin Books (N.Z.) Ltd, 182–190 Wairau Road,
Auckland 10, New Zealand

Penguin Books Ltd, Registered Offices:
Harmondsworth, Middlesex, England

First published in Penguin Books 1994

1   3   5   7   9   10   8   6   4   2

Copyright © Steve Bennett and Ruth Loetterle Bennett, 1994
All rights reserved

Illustrations by Ruth Bennett

LIBRARY OF CONGRESS CATALOGING IN PUBLICATION DATA
Bennett, Steven J., 1951–
By land, by air, by sea:the ultimate family travel activity book/
Steve & Ruth Bennett.
p.   cm.
ISBN 0 14 02.3910 3
1. Games for travelers.   2. Family recreation.   3. Travel.
I. Bennett, Ruth (Ruth Loetterle).   II. Title.
GV1206.B45   1994
794—dc20   94-26041

Printed in the United States of America
Set in ITC Garamond   Designed by Kate Nichols

Acknowledgments

A number of people made tremendous contributions during the voyage from idea to book. The indefatigable Stacey Miller once again kept our sails billowing with great ideas, inspiring us to reach our destination. Richard Freierman, who has made many a long journey with kids in tow, provided a wealth of insights and project ideas. We're also grateful to Jennifer Stoffel, the publisher of *Cleveland Parent*, for sharing her thoughts about turning vacations with kids into high adventure. Kate White, our friend and fellow parent on the go, and Dorothy Jordon, the publisher of *Traveling with Your Child*, also offered some great suggestions.

Many thanks to our editors, Nicole Guisto and Caroline White, for helping us navigate difficult shoals and keeping the project on course, and to our publisher, Kathryn Court, for her support of the project. Hats off to Roseanne Serra for her wonderful cover design, and to Kate Nichols for a splendid-looking interior design.

We're also grateful to Lynn Chu and Glen Hartley, our agents, for helping to turn this project into a reality.

Most of all, we thank our children, Audrey and Noah—great kids and great travelers—for inspiring us to embark upon this project in the first place!

Contents

1. Set the Stage

2. Home Research Bureau

3. In-House Travel Agents

4. Computer-Map Kids

5. Trip-Planning Cards

6. "Instant Expert" Cards

7. State the Facts

8. Stopover Planners

9. "Shun-piking": The Rest-Stop Alternative

10. Keeping Posted

11. Vacation Planning Central

12. Kids' Do-It-Yourself Travel Packets

13. Kids' Travel Brochure

14. Tour-Guide Preparation

15. Breaking the Language Barrier

16. Mileage Bags	17. Traveling Art Kit	18. Traveling Crayon Rubbing Kit	19. Traveling Mail Kit	20. Traveling Picture Kit

21. Travel Organizer	22. Back-Seat Drivers	23. Swiss Army Notebook	24. Card-Game Board	25. Puppets to Go

26. Deck the Road	27. Away-Time Package	28. Travel-Sticker Artists	29. Luggage Tag Factory	30. Seat-Occupied Signs

31. Family Book of Observations	32. Travel by Story	33. Family Forum: To Your Good Health!	34. Family Forum: United We Stand	35. Family Forum: When in Rome . . .

36. First-Aid Kit

37. Packing Assistants

38. It Doesn't Grow on Trees

39. We Haven't Even Left Yet!

40. Video Trip Record: Getting Ready

41. A Great Answer

42. Airplane Bag Puppets

43. Airport Find-It

44. All the Tray's a Stage

45. Alphabet Game

46. As the Crow Flies

47. Bumper Sticker Factory

48. Calcu-tainment

49. Car Counting

50. Challenging Postcards

51. Changing Scenes

52. Chrono-logical Picture Postcards

53. Codes for the Road

54. Common Threads

55. Control Tower Visit

56. Custom Car Designs

57. D=RT

58. Dots Away

59. Draw a Town

60. Draw Three

61. Drawing Around

62. Drawing Challenges

63. Entertainment Cruise

64. Esrever Gnidaer

65. First Letters First

66. Five Hundred Miles

67. Flight Map—Guess Where

68. Flying Predictions

69. Follow Me

70. From A to Z

71. Get the Picture

72. Gin Road Rummy

73. Give a Tour

74. Goofy Rules

75. Great Wiper Ensemble

76. Guess the Song

 77. Heads Up

 78. High-Flying Scavenger Hunt

 79. House Hunting

 80. How Long Would It Take?

 81. In-Flight Map Game Pack

 82. In-Flight Route Talks

 83. Land Ho!

 84. Layover Games

 85. License Plate Scrabble

 86. License to Remember

 87. List Mania

 88. Little Kids' Car Search

 89. Log Those Plates!

 90. Logos to Go!

 91. Magazine Matching

 92. Magazine Memory Circle

 93. Makes and Models

 94. Map Mavens

 95. Matching Postcards

96. Mixed-Up Seasons

97. More Map Games

98. More Word Games

99. Name Games

100. Name That Tape

101. Natural Selections

102. Nautical Careers

103. Navigator's Hat

104. Odometer Olympics

105. On the Island

106. Palindromes

107. Pass the Exits

108. Patterns

109. Pennants and Flags

110. Personalized Postcards

111. Picture Playtime

112. Puppet Road Shows

113. Reporter at Large

114. Right and Left Drawings

115. Right and Left Guess-It

116. Road Matches

117. Road Math

118. Roadside Charades

119. Scavenger Hunt at 30,000 Feet

120. Scrabble Plates

121. Sea Tales

122. See the Sequence?

123. Shape Search

124. Sign Sentences

125. Sign Word Change

126. Silence Is Golden

127. Singing in the Rain

128. Smiling Violations

129. Snork!

130. Sounds like . . .

131. Spin Those Discs

132. Start-Stop-Guess

133. This House in History

134. This Stop, Please

135. This Time Tomorrow

136. Town Anthems

 137. Town Stories

 138. Trained Guesses

 139. Travel Collage

 140. Travel Tally

 141. Traveler's Treasure Hunt

 142. Traveling Board Games

 143. Traveling Notes

 144. Traveling Shuffle Story

 145. Traveling Word Swap

 146. Tunnel Vision

 147. Under, Over, Around, and Through

 148. Vanity Plates

 149. Video Trip Record: We're on Our Way!

 150. What's Behind the Tray?

 151. What's in the Truck?

 152. What's My Job?

 153. Where on the Plane?

 154. Who's on Board?

 155. Who's Sitting Where?

156. Word Family Game

157. Word Games Galore

158. Word Games on the Go

159. Young Air Traffic Controllers

160. Your Great Photographer

161. First Impressions: The Environment

162. First Impressions: Houses

163. First Impressions: Urban Architecture

164. First Impressions: Streets and Sidewalks

165. First Impressions: Flora and Fauna

166. First Impressions: Everyday Life

167. First Impressions: Food

168. First Impressions: On the Go!

169. Camera Bugs

170. Chain Postcards

171. Sightseeing Tapes

172. Hotel Counts

173. Hotel Games

174. Just Like Home

175. Greetings from Afar

176. Look Up!

177. Map Makers

178. Historic Site Find It

179. Historic Site Queries

180. Museum Copies

181. Museum Scavenger Hunt

182. Museum Find It

183. Museum Memories

184. Other Places Rated

185. Restaurant Reviewers

186. Souvenir Scavengers

187. Daily Vacation Journal

188. Video Trip Record: There at Last!

189. Finishing-Touch Photos

190. Vacation Newsletter

191. Continuing Ed

192. Vacation Beat

193. Play It Again!

194. There's Always Next Time!

195. Family Souvenir Gallery

196. Video
Memories

197. Travel
Reviewers

198. Alphabet
Almanac

199. Friends
from Afar

200. Travel
Show-and-
Tell

201. Keeping
in Touch

202. Zany TV
Travel Report

Introduction

Land Ho!

"Why are we going there?"

"Are we there yet?"

"Oh, yuck. Who cares about seeing the old town hall? Let's watch television instead. I wish we were home."

"Where did we go again?"

Sound familiar? Traveling with kids can be the ultimate challenge for parents. Children by nature simply don't enjoy sitting still for long stretches of time. And they understandably prefer their familiar surroundings, toys, games, and friends to being away from home. But you can boost your chances of having a great vacation by getting your kids involved in the process of planning, and by having plenty of creative activities and diversions on hand while you're en route and when you reach your destination.

This book contains a broad range of activities that will engage your family throughout the entire trip; help your children to contribute ideas about where to go and what to see; pass the time in cars, planes, trains, buses, and boats; enjoy museums and appreciate the customs of the regions or foreign cultures you're visiting; and preserve the best moments of the trip once you return home.

The activities are organized into four sections:

I: Don't Leave Home without It!

Activities in this section are designed to get your children involved in trip planning. The earlier you can include your children in the planning and preparation process (by researching, offering suggestions, making checklists, and so on), the more "ownership" they'll have in the trip, and the more enthusiastic they'll be. This section is also designed to ensure that you'll have a good supply of art materials on hand, as well as several important items—such as a picture kit and an all-purpose game board—that are central to a number of the activities described in other parts of the book.

II: To and Fro.

These activities are designed to be used no matter how you are traveling. The pictures in the margin indicate whether they're best suited for travel in a car, boat, plane, or train. By making simple adjustments, you can use many of the activities in a variety of vehicles. You'll find new twists to old license-plate games, as well as a host of word games, storytelling games, map-reading projects, "in-seat" performances, and more. Whether you're waiting to board a delayed flight and need a quick activity to keep your kids from getting fidgety, or you're looking for something to get you through the last 60 miles of a long car ride, you're bound to find activities that match your children's interests.

III: There at Last!

Use these activities to enhance visits to museums, historic sites, relatives' and friends' homes, and other points of interest, and to get the most out of sightseeing. You'll also find a series of "first impression" activities that will help your kids appreciate the differences between your home and wherever you're visiting, whether you've traveled across the state line or several time zones.

IV: Home Again.

Great trips don't have to stop when you walk through the door of your home. It's tempting to dive immediately back into work and school, but by engaging in a few follow-up activities, you can seal in memories that will last a lifetime. You'll also learn some things that will help you plan successful trips in the future.

V: Resources.

A resource section at the end of the book lists a number of interesting publications, as well as some mapping software that you and your children can use with your home computer to print out custom itineraries and facts about the places you'll be visiting during your trip.

Tips for Using the Activities

Before you set out on the nation's highways and byways, set sail for distant ports, or head out to the train station or the airport, we suggest that you browse through the activities and select those that you know will be most appealing to your family during various phases of the trip. Present the ideas to your kids and let them choose the ones they like to try.

Perhaps the first thing your family should do is to jot down the activities you've selected from the book. Next, gather any materials you'll need to do them. Remember to take along your activity list, materials, and this book so you'll have everything you need to keep your travelers entertained.

The activities in this book are designed to appeal to children aged four and up, and you'll find lots of suggestions for adjusting the level of challenge to your child's skills and abilities. If you're traveling with both older and younger children, for example, and wish to do an activity involving writing skills, your older kids can act as scribes for their younger siblings. This will foster a sense of pride and ensure that younger and older kids alike are always part of the action.

As you leaf through this book, you'll notice that almost all of the activities requiring preparation and materials are located in section I. Some of the activities in section II require art supplies; if you assemble a Traveling Art Kit (activity 17) and the Swiss Army Notebook (activity 23), you'll have everything you need to do the drawing and coloring activities. For long car trips, you'll find that the Travel Organizer (activity 21) will come in handy, too.

As in all of our books, we try to downplay the competitive aspects of games and activities. Since you'll likely be sharing close quarters for a prolonged period of time while you're in transit, we feel this is especially important. If an activity involves scoring, have your kids try to beat their own previous scores rather than trying to outdo each other, or have them work together to achieve the greatest number of points for the whole family. If there has to be a winner, reward that person by allowing him or her to invent a new rule for the next game, rather than emphasizing performance and score.

And speaking of rules, while it's important to plan ahead and have a good idea of which activities you'd like to do during your trip and how you'll do them, be ready at all times to accept your children's desire to change the "rules" or to take the activity ideas and use them to create activities of their own. We'd like nothing better than to hear from you with details about a variation on one of the activities, or an activity unique to your family (see the last page of the book for our mailing address).

Finally, the goal of all travel activities is to have good, safe fun. And the key is to exercise the same judgement and common sense as you would when playing at home. When small or sharp objects are involved in arts and crafts and game activities, keep a watchful eye on young children. Also, before starting activities designed for the car, ask the driver if the games would be distracting. And in public places, be sure to accompany your children as you see fit, or to put an older, responsible sibling in charge of younger kids embarking on treasure hunts, observations, and other activities.

Enough parting words; you're probably eager to get on with your adventure. Here's to a safe and happy trip, filled with miles of family fun and happy memories in the making!

Steve Bennett
Ruth Loetterle Bennett
Cambridge, Massachusetts
May 1994

1

Don't Leave Home without It!

Set the Stage

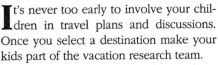

Required:
Magazines,
books

It's never too early to involve your children in travel plans and discussions. Once you select a destination make your kids part of the vacation research team.

First, find out what they know about your destination by asking them questions: "Where is it?" "What is the weather like there?" "What sorts of special attractions can we find there?" "What's the best way to get there?" etc. While everyone is talking about the trip, start jotting down questions to investigate further, along with a list of itinerary ideas.

Next, have your children look through books and magazines for photographs or advertisements that have some connection to the place where you're going. And encourage them to look through their own books as well. There may be stories that take place in the city, state, or country your family will be traveling to (see activity 32). To encourage participation, designate a bulletin board or bookshelf as your vacation information library.

**Don't Leave
Home without It!**

Who knows? Maybe the travel bureau at your destination will come to *you* for ideas and information!

Home Research Bureau

You might have a professional travel staff right under your own roof!

Have your older child visit the local library to find the addresses of the chamber of commerce, tourism office, or travel information bureau for your destination. (The librarian can steer him or her in the right direction.) While your child is there, he or she can look through travel guides for information that may come in handy on the trip. You might want to supplement the library research with an expedition to a travel agency to pick up brochures and pamphlets about your destination.

Next, have your child compose a letter or postcard to local chambers of commerce requesting information. (Younger siblings will enjoy being part of a visit to the mailbox or post office.) As information arrives, help your child write to individual institutions, such as museums and historical sites, for details.

By the time you're ready to hit the road, your child really will be an expert on your vacation destination. And what kid doesn't like getting lots of mail to boot?

***Don't Leave
Home without It!***

3 — In-House Travel Agents

Required:
Folders/large
envelopes

As your kids learn more about the places you'll be visiting, have them share their knowledge with the rest of the family. Here are some ideas to get your "in-house travel agents" started:

Dinnertime talks. Have your children pick one or two attractions to discuss at dinner. They can start the discussion by telling the rest of the family what they've learned about the place.

Home travel library. Provide large envelopes and have them sort and organize the material they've found at the library or received in the mail. Then they can label each envelope and list its contents on the outside before placing it in the household vacation library.

Guided Tour. Your kids can add some flair to their presentations by imagining that they're actually "on location," giving a guided tour for the entire family. The next stop on our tour: Niagara Falls!

*Don't Leave
Home without It!*

Computer-Map Kids

If you have a computer and a child who's adept at using it, you can enjoy some high-tech mapping fun.

A number of inexpensive atlas programs are available for both the Mac and the IBM PC. These will enable your child to learn about the places you'll be visiting. Software ToolWorks (see Resources), for example, offers a number of excellent disk-based and CD-ROM programs that allow you to create special maps showing states, portions of states, and even wall maps.

Have your child use an atlas program to create a customized map of the places you'll be visiting, and the main roads you'll be taking if you're driving. As you refine your plans, your child can print out revised maps and present them during family discussion sessions. Your child will surely take pride in being the technology wizard of the planning team.

Don't Leave
Home without It!

Trip-Planning Cards

Required:
Index cards

Does your destination boast some interesting sights and landmarks? Your family can learn enough about them before the trip to make itinerary planning a breeze.

Use the research information you've gathered (see previous activities) to identify must-see places: famous peoples' houses, presidential libraries, and other sightseeing spots at your destination. For example, in Massachusetts, you'll want to visit Plymouth Rock, the replica of the *Mayflower*, Plimoth Plantation, and so on.

Then get detailed information about each sightseeing spot. Write to the local chamber of commerce with requests for specific information, including address, directions from where you'll be staying, phone number, hours it's open to the public, and admission prices. Have your child write the key facts on index cards, arranging the cards in the order in which you'll be visiting the sites.

**Don't Leave
Home without It!**

Be sure to carry the cards with you when you hit the sightseeing road. With your cards in hand, and you can be sure that you won't arrive at a long-awaited museum five minutes before closing time!

- The Grand Canyon is 4 to 18 miles deep and 217 miles long.
- The Golden Gate Bridge, built between 1933 and 1937, spans 4,200 feet.
- The Eiffel Tower stands 984 feet tall.

Required:
Index cards, box/card file

If you're not inclined to memorize this kind of information, pass the task on to an older child. Assign him or her the job of researching interesting facts about the various sites you'll be visiting, adding the information to the trip-planning cards created in activity 5. Now your trip planning cards will have great facts as well as great directions.

Place the cards in a box (you can use a cardboard box or purchase an index-card file box at a stationery store) and let your child organize them as he or she sees fit. (Provide divider cards to help create categories.) Possible organizational schemes include alphabetical, by state, or by type of site (and so on).

Did you know that the oldest river in the country is the New River? Good thing your child plans to take a stack of "instant expert" cards along on the trip!

Don't Leave Home without It!

State the Facts

Required:

Notebook, large index cards, tabs

If your family is planning a long trip by car, you can turn every state-border crossing into an enjoyable geography lesson for your children.

After you've decided on your route, conduct some research with your kids about every state you'll be passing through. This can often be as simple as looking through an almanac or geography book at your local library. For younger kids, include tidbits like the state bird, the year the state was founded, and the state capital. Older kids can seek out such items as the state's sports teams, its noteworthy agricultural products (Vermont's maple syrup, Georgia's peaches), and its historical highlights.

Write the information in a notebook (you can give each state its own page, perhaps attaching a labeled tab to it for easy access). Then, when you reach each state's border, ask your children to tell you what they know about the state. Then add some information from your notes.

For instance, if you're entering Illinois, you might ask, "What famous house builder was born here?" The answer: Abraham Lincoln, of course!

Don't Leave Home without It!

Stopover Planners

If your kids have been helping to research the places you'll see during a car trip, why not get them involved with planning specific stops? This will make your trip diversions all the more exciting.

Use a highlighter to mark your route on a map. Assign each child a specific leg of the journey, and ask him or her to find a stopover or scenic diversion in the area. These could include historic sites, scenic vistas, natural wonders, or simply an attraction that looks too good to miss. (For long distances, can focus on finding exciting morning, afternoon, and evening stops.)

To make the activity even more interesting, plan an evening of presentations. Ask each participant to explain to everyone else why his or her stopover is a "must-see." If someone has more than one idea to present, the entire family may want to vote on the best choices.

With this activity in place, you're bound to see a bit of everything on your next road trip!

"Shunpiking": The Rest-Stop Alternative

9

There's an old tradition of bypassing the main roads for more scenic routes. Back in colonial days, instead of paying landowners a toll to cross their property, travelers "shunned" the main roads or pikes and took to the back roads instead. If you're not in a hurry to get to your destination, you can do a little "shunpiking" yourself, and sample a bit of local atmophere while you're at it.

Before the trip, visit your library to look up the names and addresses of local newspapers or county tourism offices. (The former can be found in *Editor and Publisher;* the latter will often be located in a pamphlet file.) Choose a few smaller towns or cities that you'll pass on your trip, then send out requests for a copy of either their calendar of events or a week's worth of newspapers.

Don't Leave Home without It!

As the materials arrive, search for local events that your family can enjoy during your trip. These could include strawberry socials, bake sales, auctions, flea markets, parades, fireworks displays, craft shows, and musicals. You may never take the main roads again!

Keeping Posted

The planning and anticipation for a big trip can be as much fun as the trip itself. You can tap into your kids' pretravel energy by having them make an itinerary poster to keep the vacation plans out front where everyone can see them.

Required:
Posterboard, art supplies

To begin, help your children make a large calendar on a sheet of posterboard, showing the days when your family will be on vacation. Be sure to have your kids include a few days before the trip for packing and getting ready, as well as some time afterward to settle into the house, unpack, and call friends they've missed.

Once the poster is ready, your children can fill in the specific activities and plans that you have already finalized. To make the calendar more interesting, they can add hand-drawn pictures or photos from brochures showing places you'll be visiting. Finally, they can include "wish-list" items: things that family members would like to do on vacation. (These can be added in a different color, so as not to be confused with the itinerary.)

So what's the plan for your vacation?

Don't Leave Home without It!

Vacation Planning Central

Required:

Bulletin board/
chalkboard,
pushpins/chalk

In the rush of pretrip planning, it's easy to lose or forget important items. A central-planning "command post" will ensure that nothing you need falls through the cracks.

A few weeks before your trip, get your kids involved in monitoring a vacation-planning bulletin board or chalkboard. Supply the board, as well as plenty of pushpins (exercise caution if you have small children) or chalk. Hang the board in a handy place, perhaps beside the vacation calendar (see previous activity), and at a height where everyone can reach it, then have each person make a list of items that need to be purchased or packed (see activity 37). An older child can write and post lists for younger siblings. Check off items as they are purchased or placed in the suitcase.

If you're using a bulletin board, younger kids can decorate it with trip-related pictures clipped from brochures, photos from previous vacations, or their own hand-drawn art.

Maybe this year you won't have to find a drugstore to buy Dad a toothbrush the first night of your trip!

*Don't Leave
Home without It!*

Kids' Do-It-Yourself Travel Packets

Your children can get into the spirit of the vacation by creating travel packets for the whole family.

First, provide each child with a large envelope that he or she can decorate with pictures from magazines and travel brochures and fill with:

Required:

Large envelope, art supplies, maps, index cards

Geographical Maps. Suggest that your children trace or draw maps of the places your family will be visiting, perhaps including a fantasy side trip to an imaginary place—even another planet.

Route Map. Have your children create a map showing your route. Begin by giving them an approximate idea of the route you'll be traveling, and have them plan the rest from actual maps.

Tickets. Provide cardstock or index cards for making airline, train, or boat tickets, showing the travel dates and destinations.

Picture Postcards. Provide index cards so your kids can draw your destination.

When your kids have completed their travel package, have them present it to you. It will be almost as though you're hearing about the trip for the first time!

Don't Leave Home without It!

13 Kids' Travel Brochure

Required:

Art supplies, travel brochures/ family photos, tape/glue

After you and your children have decided on a destination, why not create a travel brochure of your own to tout your choice?

First, collect brochures and other information about your intended vacation spot, from which your kids can cut out photographs. Or, they can draw pictures. If your destination is a relative's house, your children might be able to photocopy some family snapshots. Have your kids fold an 8-x-11-inch piece of paper into a three-panel brochure, then arrange and glue the illustrations onto the page. Now have your children write copy for the brochure. Prewriters might dictate the words to a family "scribe." Computer-savvy kids can word-process their entries, print them out, and glue them down in the appropriate spots.

Make sure everyone contributes to the brochure, with highlights of the destination, photograph captions, and an attention-grabbing headline.

How about having your child design this brochure: "Grandma's House—The Place to Be This Summer!"

Don't Leave Home without It!

Tour-Guide Preparation

Here's a way to get your kids ready for "duty" as tour guides at your next vacation destination.

For this activity, you'll need travel materials obtained from various state tourism offices (see activity 2 for suggestions about home travel research). Ask older children to prepare to give a guided tour by becoming the resident experts on a particular museum, historical site, or the architecture and customs of a particular city. Your kids can write down the key points on numbered index cards (perhaps keying them to a brochure) or write a script they can read when you begin your sightseeing adventures.

Tour guides can also provide commentary about the regions you're traveling through ("Upstate New York is known for . . ." or "The climate in this part of New Mexico is typically . . .").

This activity will not only help build up your children's enthusiasm about the trip, but it will be a source of pride as they display their knowledge and teach others in the family. And, who knows? It could even lead to a lifelong interest in the tourism industry!

Don't Leave
Home without It!

Breaking the Language Barrier

Buenas días. Are you and your children ready to make yourselves understood in a foreign land? *Nein?* Well, *pardonnez-moi*, but maybe you need a way to get the whole family involved in learning some basic words and phrases so you can have a *bon voyage!*

Make a visit to your local library or bookstore and look for a phrase book for the country you will be visiting. Then label objects commonly found around the house with the foreign translations, and have the whole family practice using as many of the words as possible. For things that can't be labeled easily or items you will encounter only outside, have your children draw pictures with the foreign names.

You can also have your kids make up a poster with foreign phrases that you will all want to know: "please," "thank you," "excuse me," "hello," "goodbye," "where is the bathroom?" "How do you get to . . . ," and, of course, "Do you speak English?" Hang this poster near your kitchen or dining-room table so that the entire family can practice their foreign-language skills over dinner.

Don't Leave Home without It!

Mileage Bags

Here's a twist on the time-honored practice of giving kids special snacks, small toys, and other diversions as you make your way down the highway: "mileage bags," or goodie bags dispersed after you have traveled certain predetermined distances.

Required:

Paper lunch bags, art supplies, surprises/treats

Have your children help decorate the mileage bags (paper lunch bags, actually). Then, together, decide the distance between goodie distributions, and label the bags accordingly. If, for example, you plan to travel 420 miles and you want to make up five bags, you could have your children label them 70, 140, 210, 280, and 350 miles.

Next, fill the bags with surprises. You can include snacks, small books, small toys, even coupons good for frozen yogurt at the next rest stop. When you're traveling, you'll be all set to give your kids the bags at the designated distances (you can have your children watch highway signs so they can keep track of the miles themselves).

Your kids will be glad to know that while it's 20 miles to the next rest stop, it's only 5 miles to the next mileage bag!

Don't Leave Home without It!

Traveling Art Kit

Required:

Large envelope/self-sealing plastic bags, tape and glue stick, art supplies, ruler, safety scissors

A good basic art kit is second only in importance to the first aid kit. Here's how to assemble one.

First, find a large clasp envelope or a heavy, self-sealing plastic bag to pack the different art supplies in. You will also want to have a case that will protect things and that closes securely. Your stationery or art supply store will probably sell them.

Next, stock the kit with your children's favorite art supplies. Be sure to include basics like crayons or markers, pencils, paper, safety scissors, a glue stick, tape, and a ruler. When you're shopping for the case, you may want to find some new items to add to the kit to surprise your children. Something as simple and inexpensive as a plastic stencil or a French curve will add a whole new dimension to their doodlings.

Finally, if there's room, you may want to include some heavy cardboard to use as a work surface when no desk or table is available.

Now your traveling art kit is ready. All you need are some young artists to use it!

Don't Leave Home without It!

Traveling Crayon Rubbing Kit

Here's a kit that actually grows as you travel! At each place you stop, you find or buy an inexpensive object to add to it. Here's how to get it ready.

Remove the paper sleeves from some crayons and place the crayons in a heavy, self-sealing plastic bag, along with objects suitable for rubbing, such as coins, buttons, toy medallions, or pieces of textured cloth. (Note: because small items are used, these kits are not appropriate for very young children.) You'll also need pieces of thin paper.

Your kids might start with a rubbing of some pennies and turn them into pictures of things that they see from the window. By using markers or pencils from your Traveling Art Kit (see activity 17), they'll be able to draw in features and details—perhaps adding ears, horns, a tail, and legs to turn the pennies into a pair of cows you just passed.

If your children do rubbings at regular intervals during the trip, you'll have an unusual "photo" archive of the trip ready for framing on the family gallery wall when you return home!

Required:

Crayons, paper, objects for rubbing, heavy, self-sealing plastic bag

Don't Leave Home without It!

19 Traveling Mail Kit

Required:
Clasp/string envelope, address book/ construction paper, stapler, paper, envelopes, postcards, writing supplies, stamps

Wouldn't you like to encourage your child to write home to friends and relatives during your trip? A personal letter-writing kit will help him or her to be ready and eager to keep those cards and letters going.

Fill a large clasp or string envelope with the following items:

- an address book, either store-bought or, better yet, one made by your child by folding sheets of construction paper in half and stapling them together on the fold
- a "special" pen or marker; that is, one that goes back in the envelope when it's not being used
- writing paper, envelopes, and postcards
- stamps for both letters and postcards

Don't Leave Home without It!

As you wend your way to your destination, be on the lookout for mailboxes. Unusual postmarks will add interest for friends and family as they receive letters from the road.

While you're at it, we'd really enjoy getting a letter from North Pole, Alaska (yes, there is such a place)!

Traveling Picture Kit

If you have a pile of junk-mail catalogs and circulars, old magazines and newspapers, plus double-stick tape, drawing paper, and a self-sealing plastic bag, then you have everything you need to make a picture kit for the road.

Required:
Self-sealing plastic bag, junk mail/old magazines, double-stick tape, paper

Gather the printed materials, and your child can help you clip the following types of photos:

People. Head-and-shoulders or full-length shots of politicians, sports stars, and other interesting individuals.

Scenery and buildings. Background items such as trees, houses, cars, and skyscrapers.

Miscellaneous objects. Household appliances, food, toys (look in mail-order catalogues), and other common items.

While your child assembles the kits, you can pack or do other last-minute chores. You can surely picture the benefits of that!

Don't Leave Home without It!

21 Travel Organizer

Required:

Shoebox, small cardboard boxes/plastic containers, cardboard tubes, tape, art supplies

Wouldn't you like to avoid turning around in your seat every ten minutes on a long car trip to hand your children a book, crayons, or a toy? If so, you need one or more homemade travel organizers.

Your children can make an organizer from a shoebox fitted with cardboard compartments sized to fit their needs. To begin, help your kids decide what they want to keep in the box: crayons, drawing paper, small toys, a book or magazine, and so on. Then have them create dividers for the box by gluing in smaller boxes, toilet-paper tubes, strips of light cardboard, or small plastic containers. (Be sure to have your children cut the dividers to the correct height, so that the cover will fit on the shoebox.) You can also cut a piece of heavy cardboard to fit inside the lid of the box to make a tray that can be taken out during the trip and used as a writing surface.

Finally, have your children personalize their travel organizer by decorating the lid and sides. Now stock the box with supplies. That's organization!

***Don't Leave
Home without It!***

Back-Seat Drivers

How would you like your children to help spell you at the wheel? They can in spirit, by using their own dashboards.

A junior dashboard can be as simple as a piece of cardboard with a steering wheel and dials drawn on it. Or it might have a paper plate for the steering wheel and jar or yogurt-container tops for the dials. You can make the steering wheel and dials move by bending two thicknesses of twist ties in half and balling it up at the fold, creating a "head" and two "legs." Poke the legs through a hole in the steering wheel and through the dashboard behind it. Then bend the legs outward so that the plate spins without falling off.

For a futuristic design, how about a computer screen in the center of the dash? Cut a rectangular hole in the cardboard and place a piece of colored construction paper behind it. Have your child draw on it a scene from the road, or perhaps outer space—no telling what the vehicle can really do! Bring along extra scenes and tape to give the dashboard ongoing "shelf life."

No doubt, your dashboards will give new meaning to the term "back-seat driver"!

Required:

Cardboard, markers, paper plate, jar or yogurt-container tops, twist ties, construction paper

Don't Leave Home without It!

23 Swiss Army Notebook

It's a paper holder, a playing board, a felt board, a writing surface, a traveling file, and more! To make a "Swiss Army Notebook" add the following to a smooth-surfaced three-ring binder:

Required:

Three-ring binder, paper, clasp envelopes/self-sealing plastic bags, writing supplies, felt, glue, bulldog clip, envelopes

Paper supplies. Include an ample supply of paper: lined, blank, graph, and so on.

Writing and drawing supplies. Punch three holes in a clasp envelope or self-sealing plastic bag to hold pens, pencils, crayons, and markers.

Felt board. Glue a piece of felt to the back of the notebook and cut shapes out of felt scraps to make designs. Store the shapes in an envelope.

Bulldog clip. Attach one to the top of the front cover of the notebook.

Keepsake holders. Add some empty envelopes to store ticket stubs, brochures, and guides.

You may find that this organizer is so handy you'll want one for yourself!

Don't Leave Home without It!

Card-Game Board

24

Simple games like concentration are a great way for your kids to pass the time but are difficult to play in a car, train, or plane. Here's a simple portable gameboard to make before you go (see illustration).

To make the board, first cut a 10-inch-square piece of cardboard. Then cut four 10-x-3 3/4-inch strips of construction paper and cover one side with clear adhesive covering. Fold the strips lengthwise with the adhesive covering on the outside, so that one side (or "half") measures 2 1/2 inches and the other 1 1/4 inches. Next, glue the 2 1/2-inch side to the cardboard. Staple through both sides of the strips and the cardboard at 2-inch intervals to form five pockets on each strip.

To make playing cards, have your children draw pairs of objects on the top half of thirty or so 1 1/2-x-2 1/4-inch pieces of thin cardboard. Or have them find pairs of pictures in magazines and glue them onto the upper portions of the cards. You can cover the cards with clear adhesive covering if you wish. When the preparation is done, pack everything up in a paper or plastic bag, and you're ready to roll.

Required:

Cardboard, construction paper, clear adhesive covering, glue/double-stick tape, stapler, scissors, index cards/cardstock, art supplies

Don't Leave Home without It!

Don't Leave Home without It!

25   Puppets to Go

Here's a way you and your children can make a collection of road puppets that will divert your kids' attention from the clock.

Gather the makings of puppets, including old gloves (each cut-off finger becomes a puppet), hollow rubber balls (cut a small hole in each one and poke your finger through the "head"), plastic silverware (draw a face on a spoon), mittens and socks (move your thumb up and down inside the mitten or sock to make the puppet "talk"), and paper lunch bags (put your hand inside the bottom part of the bag that's folded over and control the "mouth" with your fingers).

To make hats, hair, and costumes for the puppets, use colored paper, contact paper, cotton, yarn, felt, patches, or whatever other sewing and art supplies you have in the house. Add facial features with paint, crayons, or markers.

After you've created the puppets, place them in shoebox (which your child can decorate) for safekeeping. You might also want to bring along some extra accessories so your puppets can make quick changes en route.

Required:

Old socks, mittens, gloves, rubber balls, thin cardboard, paper bags, plastic utensils, yarn, cotton, felt and other sewing materials, art supplies

Deck the Road

Anybody can buy an ordinary deck of cards. But here's a way you and your child can make one tailored specifically for traveling.

For this activity, you'll need fifty-two index cards (or you can cut thin cardboard to the desired size). Make up a list of thirteen easy-to-draw, travel-related images, such as cars and trucks, traffic lights, gas stations, and road signs. Then choose four colors to take the place of regular card suits (hearts, spades, diamonds, and clubs). Now draw the pictures onto the cards, replicating each image four times, using a different color each time (so that every picture is now drawn in each of the four suits).

Put a rubber band around the cards and place them in your roadside travel bag or homemade organizer (see activity 21). You might also want to bring along blank cards, in case any get lost or damaged en route. Now you're set to play Gin Road Rummy (see activity 72) or any other card games your family knows.

Required:

Index cards/ cardboard, art supplies

Don't Leave Home without It!

27   Away-Time Package

Required:

Photos, drawings, mementos, box, art supplies

Has it been a while since your child last saw his or her grandparents, aunts, uncles, or other faraway relatives or friends? Before a visit, you and your child can make "away-time" packages for a special relative or friend that will fill in the blanks and let the recipient know what your child has been doing since his or her last visit.

Since this is your child's project, he or she should direct the process, identifying things that he or she wants to share that tout his or her achievements. Away-time items might include school projects (essays, poetry, arts and crafts), photos or drawings (of friends, family occasions, teachers, siblings), mementos of special occasions (ticket stubs, party hats, sea shells), and so on.

When the items are selected, help your child find a box in which everything will fit, then have him or her decorate it. Your child can now bear two gifts: himself or herself and the away-time package!

Don't Leave Home without It!

How easily can you pick out your luggage from the rest of the bags on the carousel? You should have no trouble if you have some good travel stickers.

Required:
Self-adhesive stickers, colored markers, clear adhesive covering

Supply your kids with self-adhesive labels and colorful markers, then set your children to work creating interesting travel stickers. On the serious side, your kids can draw the outlines of various states or countries they've visited or are about to visit, or simply write the names of the states in bright colors. They could also draw something that pertains to the state or country, such as main products, the official flower, or flag.

On the zany side, how about stickers obtained from a recent trip to another planet, a mythical castle, the bottom of the ocean, or the interior of a volcano?

Cover the front of the finished stickers with clear adhesive covering. Then have your children apply the stickers to the luggage.

You might get some strange looks in the baggage-claim area. But you won't have to worry about spotting your bags!

Don't Leave Home without It!

29 Luggage Tag Factory

How's your children's handwriting? Let them exercise their best penmanship with this activity—and then enjoy owning a set of custom luggage tags.

Required:

Index cards/ cardstock, art supplies, clear adhesive covering, hole punch, elastic string

Supply white or brightly-colored index cards or cardstock, trimmed to slightly less than 2 x 3 inches, and some markers. Have your children write your family's name and address and phone number.

While they're at it, your children might want to include some creative decorations on the reverse side, such as a family logo or coat of arms.

Cover the tag with clear adhesive covering on both sides and trim off the excess. Then punch a hole in one corner, pass an elastic string loop through the hole, and *voilà!* An instant luggage tag.

This activity works best if everyone will be carrying his or her own bag on the trip, but if siblings are sharing luggage, they can split the assignment so that one person does one side of the tag and the other does the reverse.

If only it were as easy to carry the luggage as it is to tag it!

Don't Leave Home without It!

Seat-Occupied Signs

If your family will be spending a lot of time on a plane or train, your children might want to make their own personalized Seat Occupied signs to bring along on the trip. They can even use them in the car to remind each other whose turn it is to sit by the window after rest stops.

Required:
Cardboard, art supplies, clear adhesive covering

Have your children make their signs on lightweight cardboard, then cover them with clear adhesive covering for durability. If you'll be traveling in foreign countries, you can have your children write the words in other languages, or use pictures that will be understood by anyone.

Encourage your children to come up with creative ideas for their signs that are friendly, funny, and have the best effect. They could, for example, have a picture of a plate of food with the words "Please don't sit on my lunch!" Or they might draw a spaceship emblazoned with the words "The occupant of this seat will beam aboard momentarily."

Whatever the sign, your children will have fun staking claim to their own small spot for the journey.

Don't Leave Home without It!

Family Book of Observations

Required:

Looseleaf binder, paper, divider tabs, art supplies

During your trip you may want to record everyone's impressions and observations (see activities 161–168). You'll be more likely to do this if you prepare a notebook ahead of time and keep it handy.

First purchase a looseleaf binder, ruled paper, and divider tabs. Then hold a family meeting during which everyone can contribute ideas about the sections that should be included: weather, food, buildings, clothing, and so on. When you've decided on the sections, older kids can label the divider tabs, and younger children can add appropriate art to the divider pages (pictures cut out of magazines or drawings of clouds for a climate section, pictures or drawings of animals for a wildlife section, and so on).

During the trip, when someone says, "That's the most beautiful flower I've ever seen!" he or she will have a section in the notebook in which to record the memorable sight.

One last thing: Don't forget to pack the book!

Don't Leave Home without It!

Travel by Story

What better time to read *Make Way for Ducklings*, or another book that takes place in Massachusetts, than right before your family takes a trip to Boston.

Required:
Children's books

Find and bring along one or more storybooks that take place in the city, state, or country you're visiting. Here are some books to consider: *Cable Car and the Dragon* (if your destination is San Francisco), *The Adventures of Paddington* (if you're headed for London), the Madeline series (if you're touring Paris), and *Babar Comes to America* (which mentions a number of U.S. cities in between New York and Los Angeles).

Before you reach your destination, read the book aloud, emphasizing the parts of the story that relate to the places your child can visit. When you arrive, your family can trace the path that the storybook characters took: walking along a particular trail, visiting historical landmarks, touring museums, and so on.

Later, family members can compare the storybook characters' fun with your own. So, which would your child rather be: a duckling residing in the Boston Public Garden or a young tourist?

Don't Leave Home without It!

Family Forum: To Your Good Health!

No one likes to think about illnesses or accidents, but a family safety meeting can help make everyone's vacation as safe and pleasurable as possible, and without alarming your kids. This can be especially important if you're traveling to another country, which may have health issues different from our own.

First, make a trip to the library or ask your family physician for specific information about the health problems you may encounter on your trip. Find out about drinking water, pasteurization of milk, problematic insects, etc.

Share the information during a family forum and create a list of rules for staying healthy and happy while you're away. Use the meeting to discuss what is done to the water your family drinks at home, what pasteurization means, and so on.

Don't Leave Home without It!

As you create your travel rules, older children can write them up and place them on the vacation bulletin board (see activity 11). The first rule might be: "Only drink bottled water." The second might be: "Wear sunscreen from 10:00 in the morning till 3:00 in the afternoon." And, of course, "Eat an apple a day"!

Family Forum: United We Stand

How good are your kids at sticking together in crowds and paying attention to landmarks? Sometimes it's hard to concentrate on where you are when there is so much that is new and unusual. Here's an idea that will help put everyone's mind at ease about getting lost, without causing fear and dampening the vacation enthusiasm.

Required:
Baseball caps, glow-in-the-dark paint or glue

If you don't already have a distinctive, brightly colored baseball or other cap for each child, purchase one. Then set your kids to work personalizing their caps for the trip using glow-in-the-dark glue or paint (either can be found in craft stores) to draw a distinctive picture or symbol. (For security reasons, don't have your child write his or her name or initials.)

While you're decorating your hats, discuss the importance of sticking together, how the caps will help all of you spot each other, and what to do if someone should get separated. Keep the discussion light and nonthreatening.

Now everyone can rest a bit easier. But before you pack away the hats, slip outside in the dark and watch each other glow.

Don't Leave Home without It!

Family Forum: When in Rome . . .

Often, kids expect that people in other cultures live just as we do. Here's a way to clue in your child on different customs, practices, and etiquette that he or she might encounter.

Spend some time at the library looking into the cultural differences and practices of your destination, particularly as they pertain to children. Then write down a list of differences that you feel are important. For instance, in Europe children are expected to give up their seats for adults on buses; in many parks you're not supposed to walk on the grass; and don't expect ice water in restaurants unless you specifically ask for it.

During a family forum, discuss the fact that cultures include rules or conventions that everyone follows so that they get along with each other. Then talk about each of the differences you have identified, comparing them with some rules of our culture that your family thinks are important.

Make the session fun and entertaining, and your kids may learn enough to be mistaken for locals!

Don't Leave Home without It!

First-Aid Kit

Everyone should have a first-aid kit when they travel, so why not have your kids assemble one with you?

Supply a small box and have your child tape or glue in cardboard divider or tubes custom-fit to hold the following (see activity 21 for other suggestions on making box dividers):

- Assorted bandages
- First-aid cream
- Gauze and sterile pads
- Acetaminophen (in childproof bottles)
- Antibiotic ointment
- Tweezer
- Q-tips
- Hydrogen peroxide
- First-aid tape
- Elastic bandage
- Small scissors

Your child can decorate the box with a red cross, pictures of a doctor, or anything else that seems appropriate. Hopefully, you won't need to tend to any injuries while you're traveling. But if you do, you and your children will be prepared.

Required:

Small cardboard box, miscellaneous pieces of cardboard, glue/tape, first-aid supplies

Don't Leave Home without It!

Packing Assistants

Required:

Paper, pencil, clipboard/ vacation central planner (see activity 11)

Does your family delay packing until the very last minute? Whatever your packing habits, here's a simple way to get your whole family to pitch in.

During a family forum, discuss the items you'll be taking along, from clothes to teddy bears to bedtime books. An older child can write up or word-process a list. Keep the list on a clipboard or affixed to the Vacation Central Planner (see activity 11).

On packing day, set aside a single bag for each child to fill himself or herself (even a small suitcase or knapsack will give a child a sense of importance); if everyone is sharing a bag, have people stack the items they're taking in a corner of their room. An older child can check off the items as they're placed in the suitcases.

This activity may do more than prevent you from forgetting a key article of clothing or accessory. When your kids try to lift all the items they want to take, they might quickly decide that they really don't need fifteen stuffed dinosaurs or ten sweaters!

Don't Leave Home without It!

It Doesn't Grow on Trees

Here's how you can encourage your child to budget his or her travel cash and take pride in the accomplishment.

First establish a spending limit with your child. Then have your child consider what purchases he or she might want to make during the trip: postcards, souvenirs from museum gift shops, and so on.

Required:
Small notebook, pencil

Help your child use this wish list to come up with a budget, determining how much money he or she can spend in each expense category. Then have your child transfer into an "accounting" notebook all the information: total budget, desired items, projected costs, and expense categories. The figures in each category are then tallied and added together to make sure your child is within budget.

After each purchase, your child fills in the amount spent and deducts it from the category and budget totals. Be as flexible as you can about allowing some unbudgeted purchases. After all, when is the next time your child will have a chance to buy an authentic brontosaurus toothbrush!

Don't Leave Home without It!

We Haven't Even Left Yet!

39

You know that sooner or later you'll hear the dreaded, "Are we there yet?" or "How long until we get there?" How about coming up with some really creative answers for this trip in advance, based on your child's own experience? This will help give your child a meaingful sense of time, and provide some amusement as well.

Before you leave, get into the habit of timing the activities that take place during a typical week in your child's life, or jotting down time spans that your child knows, such as the length of classes and sports games.

Include actions such as brushing teeth, getting dressed, eating breakfast, walking to school, doing chores around the house, and walking to a friend's house. Make a list for yourself with the activities and how long they take, but don't tell your child what it's for.

When your list is ready, stash it away with your car supplies. Then, when the infamous question arises, turn to activity 41, pull out your list, and offer some brilliant answers!

Don't Leave Home without It!

Video Trip Record: Getting Ready

Don't wait 'til you hit the road to begin videotaping your trip!

Older kids can tape trip preparations and conduct interviews, and younger children will have lots to say about what they're doing to get ready to travel. How about including these predeparture segments on your vacation video:

Required:
Video camera

Family planning meetings. Keep the video camera running when your family sits down to discuss the upcoming trip.

Interviews. Have your family members take turns being the designated videotaper so that everyone gets a chance to be on camera and to describe what he or she is looking forward to about the trip.

Packing chronicles. Get that camera out when everyone is struggling to make all his or her stuff fit into suitcases. Have your kids describe what they're bringing and why, and be sure to include mom and dad trying to fit it all in the car!

See activities 149, 188, and 196 for suggestions about making an ongoing video record as you travel.

Don't Leave Home without it!

II

To and Fro

"**A**re we there yet?"

Younger children often don't have the fine-tuned sense of time required to fully understand a straightforward answer. But if you timed some of your children's familiar activities (see activity 80) before you left, you offer some interesting equivalencies.

If you don't have prepared times, just use activities you know have set times (classes, sports practices, etc.). First make a list of the activities; then draw a line of boxes next to each entry. Each box represents doing the listed activity once, and the entire line of boxes will represent your total trip time.

Now, when your children ask how long it will be until you arrive, you can have them check off the time you've already traveled in equivalent activities, and they'll be able to relate the time remaining to things they do often.

"Are we there yet?" "No, but it looks like we'll be there in six toothbrushings, one school recess, and three trips to the library."

To and Fro

Airplane Bag Puppets

With any luck, your children will not need the airsickness bags—except for making some puppets. (You might want to ask the flight attendant for extra bags, just to be on the safe side.)

Required:
Art supplies

Your children can make puppets out of the bags by simply drawing on faces, hair, and clothes using crayons or markers. If you have put together a Traveling Art Kit (activity 17), your children can make more sophisticated puppets by cutting out and pasting on clothing and features using construction paper, yarn, cotton, felt, and whatever other materials you've included in the kit.

You might find other interesting add-ons, such as ready-made faces and outfits, in airline magazines or other magazines purchased at the newsstand before you departed. Your children can cut them out and glue them onto the puppets.

When your kids have completed their puppets, have them pull down a tray table and use it for a stage. Great performances are literally in the bag!

To and Fro

43 Airport Find-It

If you find yourselves stuck for an hour or more at the airport, here's an activity that can help you pass the time.

Accompany your child as he or she tries to find as many of the following types of items as you can:

- things with the airline's logo on it
- the nearest bathroom
- a free ride (such as bus service between terminals)
- the best view of the runway (Is there an observation tower?)
- free entertainment (Is there a children's area with toys or climbing structures?)
- a specific word or number

How about this one: The best way back to your gate. Does anyone remember the number?

All the Tray's a Stage

Do you spend the better part of most flights with your youngest child on your lap? If so, you'll appreciate this simple and entertaining finger-puppet show, which is bound to amuse your toddler.

Required:
Puppet-making materials, bandages/napkins

You can plan ahead by bringing along some finger puppets (you can make them out of the fingers from old gloves, strips of paper, or even bandages). You can also create your own characters on the fly by draping small squares of paper napkin over your fingertips, securing them with a rubber band or piece of tape around the puppets' "waist," and drawing on faces. You can also, of course, draw faces right on your fingers.

When your cast of characters is ready, reach your hands under the tray table so that your fingers stick up in full view of your child. And on with the show!

To and Fro

Alphabet Game

Here's a simple word game that puts a new twist on making an alphabetical list of items. The longer the game goes on, the more there is to remember, and the harder it gets.

One player starts by saying a word that starts with *A*. (You and your children can decide beforehand if you want to limit the choice of words—for example, to travel in general, or to the specific kind of traveling you are doing.) The next player repeats the *A* word, then adds one that starts with *B*. The third repeats the growing list, then adds a *C* word, and so on. For example, the first player may say "automobile." Player two might say "automobile, bus." Player three might say "automobile, bus, car," and so on, until the list gets too long to remember.

You can allow players to skip difficult letters like J, Q, X, and Z. And for a variation, have your kids try to do the alphabet backwards.

Now, let's see: what might such a list be like on a plane? How about "airport, blankets, cargo hold, doors, emergency exit, flaps . . ."

As the Crow Flies

Here's an advanced map game that should tickle the fancy of kids able to read map legends.

Required:
Road maps

Make sure that each player has a map, and have him or her check it for clear markings of topography such as rivers, lakes, dams, and mountains. Ask participants to find the place where you are currently, as well as your destination.

Then ask everyone to find the shortest route between the two points. Do all the players come up with the same path? Are you taking the best possible route? If you keep to that route, how many miles would you have to travel today to arrive at your destination on time?

Next, ask your navigators to imagine they can magically drive through such obstacles as mountains and rivers. How much traveling time would that save? What different sights would that enable you to see? If you had a magical vehicle that changes depending upon the topography, when would it change into a plane, a boat, a car, or a train for the quickest and most comfortable trip ever? Maybe your kids could send their findings to an innovative car manufacturer!

To and Fro

Bumper Sticker Factory

Required:
Paper,
art supplies

Some travelers like to collect souvenir bumper stickers on their journeys. But why not make your own? All the better to remember where you've been on your vacation.

Cut bumper-sticker-sized strips of plain white paper and provide some art supplies. Now your kids are ready to open their own bumper-sticker manufacturing plant.

Each traveler can make his or her own bumper sticker, or teams can work together (for example, one person might draw the pictures while another writes the text). The bumper stickers can include the name of a city, town, or state you're passing through; a logo or design (perhaps an indigenous tree or a house built in the local architectural style); or a slogan (one that says something about the economy, for example).

Who knows? If you pass through any places with exotic names like Essex (Vermont) or Lebanon (New Hampshire), you might even be able to convince your friends back home that you traveled out of the country!

Calcu-tainment

For the price of a burger and fries, you can buy a calculator. Why not get one for each passenger in the car and try some of these games?

Required:
Calculator

A round of math. Take turns calling out simple numbers and operations. The first person might say "seven plus eight," and everyone enters it. The next might say "plus thirty-seven," and so on. After five minutes (or five miles), see if everyone has the same answer.

Quick solve. Call out a math problem and see who can solve it.

Percentages. Explain percentages and have your kids calculate what percentage of the trip you've traveled so far.

Miles per gallon. Keep track of your gas usage for a leg of the trip, then see if players can calculate your mileage.

Younger kids will no doubt enjoy the calculators too. In no time at all they'll have decided it's something exotic, like the control panel for their spaceship!

To and Fro

49 Car Counting

Your car might be a four-door, six-cylinder, five-passenger sedan, or a two-door, four-cylinder, eight-passenger minivan. In either case, your vehicle also includes a host of the other things that your children can count and catalog.

Have your kids create their own lists based on counting objects in your car. Suggest a category, such as everything that's used to control the car (steering wheel, brake pedal, gas pedal, shift) or things in cars that make passengers more comfortable (heater, armrests, headrests, window controls). Then have your children tally away.

Other possible counting categories include objects that go on and off, lights, things that only the driver can use, and even things that probably shouldn't be in a car (like cracker crumbs left on the floor by a younger sibling).

When your kids think they've listed every possible thing to list and count in the car, see who can come up with just one more category to tabulate: how much fun you're having!

Challenging Postcards

If you received a postcard that didn't have a return address on it, could you guess where and whom it came from?

Required:
Art supplies

Have each traveler make a postcard that pictures a building, river, mountain, or something else you've passed in your travels. Older participants can also write a related message ("There are as many skyscrapers here as there are big apples"), leaving out the name of the actual place. Address the postcard to a fellow passenger and "mail" it (hand it across the seat).

Recipients then try to guess the name of the city, state, or country where the postcard "originated." Pre-readers can rely on the picture alone. Others can name a place based on the drawing (perhaps cross-referencing it with pictures in a guide book), read the messages, and amend their guesses, if necessary. Stumped? Then describe the picture and read the message aloud to other family members, and see who can guess the correct "mystery postcard" origin!

To and Fro

51 Changing Scenes

Required:
Art supplies

What catches the attention of each member of your family? Find out with this activity.

Supply each passenger with paper and writing supplies. Then call out "draw," at which point everyone looks out the window and sketches one object that he or she sees. Wait a certain interval, then say "draw" again. The interval can be based on time, distance, or even road signs (everyone draws again when the next exit sign appears). If you're traveling by train, you can base the intervals on station stops. By air, each person sitting next to a window can try to find a shape in the clouds to draw, or perhaps sketch an interesting land form.

When the game is over, have everyone compare their artwork. There are bound to be a few surprises about what different people chose to draw. Now that's strange . . . how come you're the only one who sketched the UFO beaming up the herd of cows outside of Chicago?

Chronological Picture Postcards

Traveling not only exposes us to new experiences, but it also treats us to a series of novel images. Can your kids put these images (captured on postcards) in chronological order?

Required:

Picture postcards, art supplies

While en route to your destination, passengers collect picture postcards in various places or participants can make their own postcards that picture a noteworthy building, tourist attraction, or the like. (Write a number on the blank side of the postcards you buy or make them so you can later verify the correct order.)

Once you have a stack of postcards, family members take turns putting them in order without peeking at the numbers. Challenge players to beat the clock, or see whether your kids can work together to improve on their previous time. For the ultimate test, try to arrange the postcards in reverse order.

Older siblings or grownups can coach younger children by asking questions like "Can you find the amusement park we visited?" and "Where are the orange groves we saw next?"

So, after you saw the Golden Gate Bridge, what did you do for an encore?

To and Fro

53 Codes for the Road

Required:
Paper
Writing supplies
Road map

Do your children like secret messages? If so, they can create their own secret codes using the symbols on a road map.

Have your kids start by writing the alphabet down the left side of a page in a single column. Then have them scour a road map and look for symbols to use as replacements for letters. Their selection could be random, or they could try to find symbols to match the letters. For example, an → could be used for *A*, ⋔ for *P*, ★ for *S*, ◉ for *E*, and ① for *I*. Have your kids write the code substitutions to the right of each letter of the alphabet. Once your children have their secret code established, they can write each other cryptic messages.

It's easy to adjust the activity to the age of your children by varying the difficulty of the codes. For beginning readers, you might want to substitute just a letter or two. Older kids may want to try substitutions for the whole alphabet! "★o h→v◉ a gr◉→t t①m◉, k①d★!"

To and Fro

Common Threads

If your kids enjoy guessing games, then this activity will probably be a hit with them. The object of the game is to have one person list items that fit an unnamed category and have everyone else try to figure out what the category is.

Let's say that the child giving the clues is thinking of the category "things with wheels." He or she might list "bicycle," "roller skates," "cars," "trucks," "airplanes," and "shopping carts." After each clue is given, everyone gets a chance to guess the category, and the first one to get the right answer goes on to give the next set of clues.

As a variation for older children, you can have players limit their clues to things they see from the car or train that fit the secret category.

Okay, what category do these fall under: "Buy souvenirs," "eat at restaurants," "visit museums," "collect seashells," "take day hikes," and "stay in hotels or motels." Give up? It's "things we like to do on vacation!"

To and Fro

Control Tower Visit

Most airports have a public observation area in or near the control tower. What a great place to pass the time during a layover!

After you've spent a little time looking at what's happening on the runway, try this guessing game with your kids. Give them some questions to ponder, then have them predict what's going to happen.

Here are some starter questions: How many planes will land in the next 60 seconds? How many green suitcases will be unloaded from a particular plane? Which airline has the most planes visible? How long will it take a particular plane to take off once it leaves the gate?

You can also have your children do some simple tallies, counting such things as how many planes take off in a 10-minute period, how many minutes there are between landings, or how many rental cars drive by in a given amount of time.

You can even have them try to spot your luggage as it gets loaded onto the plane. Hey, wait! That's the wrong plane!

Custom Car Designs

Alfter you've been traveling for a while, you might wish your car had wings, a souped-up engine, or some other fantastic design alteration. What can your kids think of to improve your car?

Encourage your children to think of things to make the car faster, safer, more comfortable, better looking, and perhaps even better smelling. Your kids can keep a list of their ideas, and even turn them into drawings. Here are some ideas for equipping the greatest car ever:

- flotation pontoons for crossing rivers
- a bathtub, so you can arrive refreshed
- helicopter blades on the roof, for flying over traffic jams
- twelve more wheels, for a smoother ride
- a rose garden growing out of the trunk
- grass on the roof to keep the car cool
- an ejector seat and parachute

After your kids have finished modifying the car, you can have them think of an appropriate (or silly) name for their new vehicle. Then your family can complete their trip in the marvelous Grass-Domed River Jumper!

To and Fro

57 D=RT

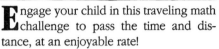

Engage your child in this traveling math challenge to pass the time and distance, at an enjoyable rate!

The game is based on the simple formula Distance = Rate x Time. For example, if you travel at 60 miles per hour for two hours, you will travel 120 miles, because 60 x 2 = 120. (The formula can also be expressed as "Rate = Distance ÷ Time" and "Time = Distance ÷ Rate.")

To play, pose some problems based on your travel speed. For example, ask your child how long it will take to go 150 miles at 50 miles per hour. You can also relate the problems to mileage signs you pass: If your destination city is 90 miles away, how long will it take to get there at 60 miles per hour? For a twist, have your child include the time spent at rest stops to determine your average speed for the trip.

Now when he or she asks "How far is it?" you can answer, "Go figure!"

To and Fro

Dots Away

All you need to play this game is a sheet of paper and a pencil. You can make it as simple or as challenging as you like, and once your kids get started, they can play with each other for miles of smiles.

Required:
Writing supplies

Make a grid of dots on a piece of paper, either plain or graph. The more dots you place on the grid, the more challenging the game becomes. A good starting size to teach your kids the game is a grid of six dots by six.

The game is played by connecting two adjacent dots with a line. Each player in turn adds a new line to the grid, trying to avoid creating a three-sided box that the other player can "capture" in his or her next move. Every time a player adds a fourth side and closes a box, he or she marks it with his or her initial. Whoever has the most boxes in the end wins.

This could be one time when you actually do want to get yourself into a box!

To and Fro

59 Draw a Town

Required:
Road map,
paper,
art supplies

Have you ever stopped to wonder how a lot of towns got their names? Take a close look at a map, and you may find some names that are pretty unusual!

Have your children pick some interesting names from the map and try to draw how they imagine the towns would look if they resembled their names. Maybe they'll end up with a giant chocolate bar for Hershey, Pennsylvania.

What about Marblehead, Massachusetts; Great Neck, New York; Little Rock, Arkansas; Forest Hills, New York; Tarzana, California; Buffalo Grove, Illinois; Rolling Meadows, Illinois; Thousand Oaks, California; Appleyard, Washington; Grapeland, Texas; Bowling Green, South Carolina; Harmony, Rhode Island; Tripp, South Dakota; Musselshell, Minnesota; Eagle Rock, Virginia; Tuba City, Arizona; Buccaneer Estates, Florida; Garden City, Kansas; Tombstone, Arizona; and Big Horn, Wyoming?

These are just some of the obvious ones. What do you suppose your children will draw for Apopka, Florida?

To and Fro

Draw Three

Here's an activity sure to keep everyone's mind off the time. Write down twenty to thirty place names on small pieces of paper and put them in a small bag. Limit the places to those you will be visiting, or at least driving near, during your trip.

Required:
Writing supplies, paper bag, road map

Each child pulls three pieces of paper from the bag and uses a road map to discover the following information about the places named: Which two places are closest together?; Which is farthest north? The largest?; The smallest?; The closest to where you are?; The closest to your home town?

After your kids have answered all the questions, have them pick the next three slips of paper from the bag—they can either start fresh with those, or answer the questions again for all six locations.

For a silly twist, you can have them make up their own questions and answers: Which city has the most green cars with orange stripes?

To and Fro

61 Drawing Around

Required:
Paper,
art supplies

The family that travels together draws a picture together!

Place a sheet of paper on a clipboard or other hard surface that can be passed from person to person, and then have passengers take turns drawing. The first artist looks for one item (a barn, river, animal, mountain, bridge, building) in the passing scenery and then sketches it. The next artist spots another object and adds it to the drawing, and so on. Each person should add his or her contribution in such a way that all the objects fit together to create a coherent picture.

For a variation, give each child a piece of paper and have him or her draw a separate picture. Each artist takes turns calling out items that everyone has to include in the drawing. When the pictures are done, pass them around and see just how different they turned out.

There's more than one way to sketch a cow, an ocean, and a Buick in the same drawing!

To and Fro

Drawing Challenges

What's important here isn't what you draw; it's how you draw it. Pass out art supplies or have your kids use their Swiss Army Notebook (see activity 23) to draw the following:

Required:
Paper,
art supplies

One line only. Pick an object you see out the window and draw it without lifting the pencil off the page.

In the dark. Have your children draw with their eyes closed.

Wrong hand. Have your children draw by holding their pencils in the hand they normally don't write or draw with.

Buddy drawings. Have each child start a picture. Call "switch" at regular intervals, and have the artists swap pictures and continue drawing.

Command Performance. With his or her eyes closed, one child follows another child's verbal drawing instructions (draw a circle, a horizontal line, an oval, etc.).

Be sure to keep your children's masterpieces. When you get home, create a Road Art Exhibition and reap the artistic benefits of your industrious trip!

Socks by Sam

To and Fro

63 Entertainment Cruise

Required:
Paper,
writing supplies

Taking a ferry or boat ride somewhere? Once the novelty wears off, your kids might be longing for dry land. Here are a few shipshape activities that can help you keep your kids occupied until you reach the pier (your supervision required).

Countoff. Count: other boats, snoozers, people with baseball caps, people feeding sea gulls, number of buoys passed, and so on.

Snack-bar monitors. Keep track of people coming and going at the snack bar: who buys a hot dog, who stays at a table rather than going on deck, how many people are on line at a given time, and so on.

Boat math. Figure out how fast the boat is going by asking the crew the cruising time and distance (rate = time ÷ distance).

So what's the most popular snack food among the under-16 crowd on your boat?

To and Fro

Esrever Gnidaer

Esrever ni sngis yawhgih daer ot ekil dnuos ti dluow tahw? Oops! Make that "What would it sound like to read highway signs in reverse?" The answer is clearly, "Pretty silly!" But it makes for a great highway game.

Demonstrate to your children how to read exit signs, billboards, truck lettering, store signs, and anything else they can find, backward. It's easier to start with if they jot down the words on a piece of paper before reading it backwards; then they can try it from memory alone. They'll quickly discover that some of the "words" they come up with may sound like real words.

Once your kids get the hang of the strange pronunciations, they can make the game more interesting by coming up with silly definitions to go with the nonsense words they've discovered. They might just create their own secret language (even if nobody knows what anyone else is saying).

Pay attention: "Daeha sevruc"! And above all, "Pirt ecin a evah."

To and Fro

First Letters First

Road signs don't just direct or welcome us; they also launch some fun traveling games!

When you spy a road sign that contains the name of a city or state, read it aloud. Fellow passengers then take turns coming up with other cities, states, countries, and continents that begin with the same letter. For example, suppose you see a sign that reads, "Welcome to Walla Walla." Your traveling companions might suggest Winnipeg, Wisconsin, Waikiki, the West Indies, and so on. Alternatively, players might offer places that begin with the *last* letter of the designated place. When no one can think of any further places that begin with that letter, choose another sign and start all over.

WAIKIKI!

As a variation, you can have each traveler write down a list of all the places they can think of that start with the chosen letter. Players then compare lists and see who thought of the most places, or whose places were the most exotic. You can also up the challenge by adding a time limit.

Did anybody else think of Wessex (an old Anglo-Saxon kingdom in England) or Ahmadabad (a modern-day city in India)?

To and Fro

Five Hundred Miles

A re your traveling companions in the mood for a game of blackjack? Here's a variation tailor-made for the road.

The object of the game is to accumulate as close to five hundred points or miles as you can without going over. To begin, "deal" each player one "card" (i.e. read the numbers on exit, route, and other signs). The first player then "draws" another "card" (i.e. call out the number of the next sign), then the next player takes a turn, and so on, until everyone has two "cards," and the round is over. Subsequent rounds alternate dealing and drawing cards in the same way.

Players keep track of their total "card" values using scrap paper and a pencil (older players can help junior players with the math). When players accumulate as close to five hundred points as they believe possible, they say "freeze." The "dealer" then bypasses the "frozen" players while the others take their turns. Once the last draw is done, see who really was closest to five hundred.

Or try playing in teams—it shouldn't take long to travel five hundred miles!

Required:
Writing supplies

To and Fro

Flight Map—
Guess Where

Those route maps in complimentary airline magazines can be a good source of entertainment for you and your kids. Try this clue-and-guessing game for starters (see activities 81 and 82 for other airline-map games).

To begin, make sure each family member has a copy of the magazine and has opened it to the route maps. Then, give your kids clues about places that are named on the map (cities, states, or countries), and have them try to guess the locations. For instance, you might say, a state with a warm climate, nearly surrounded by water (Florida) or the city on a Great Lake with the most route connections (Chicago).

Gear the clues to your children's ages by either limiting the information to things they can find on the map or including things they're likely to know about various cities and states, like where the Statue of Liberty is located.

Now, I'm thinking of a city that is home to a mom who plays great games with her kids on airplanes . . .

To and Fro

Flying Predictions

How often has your family rushed to get to the airport an hour before departure time only to find out that your flight has been delayed? Next time that happens, try playing this guessing game.

Ask airport- or airplane-related questions and solicit your children's best answers. A great starter question is: "How soon will the next plane land?" or "When will the flight attendant come by next?" (if you're on the plane, perhaps waiting for takeoff). In either case, if the question involves time and you don't have a watch, your kids can count, "One hippopotamus, two hippopotamus," and so on to see how accurate their guesses are.

Your children can also come up with predictions before takeoff that can be answered once you've boarded the plane. For example, "How many passengers will be carrying attaché cases?" "What will they serve for the in-flight meal?" or "How long will the flight take?"

If only your kids could accurately guess the answer to this question: Is there any chance that your plane will land on time?

To and Fro

Follow Me

Required:
Two copies of a map

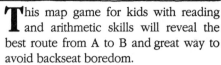

This map game for kids with reading and arithmetic skills will reveal the best route from A to B and great way to avoid backseat boredom.

To do this activity, you'll need two copies of the same map, preferably for the area you are driving through. Make sure the maps indicate the miles between cities or towns, or between exits. Give one map to your child and keep one for yourself. Starting at an easy-to-find location (point it out to your child), give travel directions based on the roads, landmarks, intersections, and mileage shown on the map (you might have to point out the mileage numbers on the various road segments).

For example, you might say, "Take I-80 west for 15 miles; take Route 4 north to the next town; take Route 11 toward the lake for 7 miles." Then ask your child where he or she is on the map, and see if you have both "arrived" at the same location!

To and Fro

As a variation, have your child pick the route for you to follow. You can point out a destination on the map and have your child give directions to get there.

Just follow the directions to fun ahead!

From A to Z

Here's a simple word game that's well suited for young readers. It's easy to play anywhere, and it can be put aside and returned to later in the trip.

Required:
Writing supplies

The object of the game is to write an alphabetical word list (exclusive of particularly tough letters like Q, X, and Z). The first time through the list, every word should be one syllable long. The second time, use only two-syllable words. Third round, the words must be three syllables. The game can be played individually with each player making his or her own list, or as a group collaborating on a single list.

As a variation, you could have your children try to use words relating to things you drive past or actions taking place outside. You could make the game more difficult for older children by not allowing proper nouns and not allowing words to be reused in a different form (for example, if the first list has "take," the second list could not have "taking").

So, ant, apple, antelope, arithmetic—and away we go!

To and Fro

71 Get the Picture

Required:
Paper/
cardboard,
magazines/
picture books

Sometimes a limited view of the big picture can yield hilarious results, as in this guessing game you can play with your child. (For a real-world version of this game, see activity 146).

To play, you cover a picture in a magazine or a book with a sheet of paper or cardboard that blocks out all but a few small sections, then have your child try to guess the big picture.

To create the cover sheet, make a series of uneven folds in a piece of paper, then cut off half-inch pieces along the edges of the folds. When you unfold the paper, it will have holes in it. The fewer holes you make, the more of the picture will be covered. As an alternative, you can make a set of cardboard cover sheets with viewing holes before you leave home. You should make at least three sizes: 3 x 5 inches, 4 x 6 inches, and 8 x 10 inches.

When you're ready to play, simply grab a magazine or book, cover a picture in it, and pass it to your child so that he or she can try to describe the big picture.

Gin Road Rummy

Here's a card game tailored for traveling and for using your Deck the Road cards (see activity 26).

As in traditional gin rummy, the dealer gives each person seven cards.

Players arrange their cards in the usual rummy way, placing side by side the cards with like pictures (for instance, all of the stoplights go together). To win, a player has to get three cards with one type of picture and four cards with another. If anyone is dealt a winning hand initially, he or she says "gin" and helps the dealer for the rest of the round.

As a variation, try this: let the number of cards that each player receives from the dealer be determined by the number of people in the next car you pass (or that passes you). After receiving the cards, the player places at the bottom of the deck the same number of cards from his or her hand. Then it's the next player's turn, and so on. At any point during the game, a player says "gin" when he or she has a winning hand.

Gin rummy was never this much fun before!

Required:

Homemade cards (see activity 26)

To and Fro

73　Give a Tour

Required:

Cardboard tube/rolled-up paper

Could your child be a great tour guide? Find out with this activity.

Give your child a "microphone" (a paper-towel tube or a rolled-up piece of paper), and he or she can tell you about your surroundings, directing you to look out one of the windows to see imaginary creatures, buildings, and people.

One easy guided-tour theme is *"homes of the famous."* Your child points out houses and buildings and tells which sports stars, politicians, writers, and other famous people live in each.

Another is *"history trail"* with land-marks like the first tree to be tapped for maple syrup, and the little-talked-about Vermont log cabin that Lincoln built.

Finally, how about *"exotic zoo,"* featuring unusual animals, birds, fish, and other creatures that you "see" during your ride.

Your child can also add real sightseeing attractions to the tour. Passengers can then look out the window to check which items are real and which are imaginary.

Who knows? Maybe there really *is* a dinosaur grazing in the corn field.

To and Fro

Goofy Rules

Rules, rules, rules! Every interesting new place your children go to during your vacation probably comes with a new set of rules. Here's an opportunity for your kids to make up their *own* zany rules and spot violators. For instance:

In a hotel. How about "No bungee jumping in the lobby" or "Guests must keep pet kangaroos off the beds."

At a campground. What about "Do not eat the boulders." Maybe they'd completely ignore "Swimmers must remain on the beach."

In an airplane. Can you imagine "No wing-walking during takeoffs and landings?"

On a boat. How about "Please do not kiss the squids" or "Lifeboats may be used on dry land only!"

Once your kids have made up their rules, they can devise fines and penalties for scofflaws. Watch out! You may find yourself taking a long walk on a short plank!

To and Fro

Great Wiper Ensemble

Maybe you can't fit a twelve-piece orchestra in your car, but you can certainly enjoy the next-best thing: a set of windshield wipers!

Let the rhythm of the windshield wipers set the pace for a stellar family performance. Each of the passengers chooses a sound: hand clapping, toe tapping, box thumping, or vocalizing a syllable such as "ah," "eee," or "hoo"). You assign each person a time and frequency to make the sound (based on the windshield wipers' rhythm; for example, a "musician" might clap in time to each windshield-wiper beat or tap his or her toe on every other beat).

Each person practices making his or her sound alone; then the whole family performs together. A designated "musician" begins by making a sound. At the signal, the next player jumps in, then the next, and so on, until the entire ensemble is "making music." See how long the family chorus can keep time to the windshield wipers (when players get confused, simply stop the "music" and begin again).

With practice (and a bit of rain), your family members may soon have your car sounding like Symphony Hall!

To and Fro

Guess the Song

Shazam! Your family's favorite melodies have just been transformed into a challenging guessing game.

One person is the "hint-giver." He or she thinks of a tune that the other passengers know. Your family can also write song titles on slips of paper and put them in a bag; then, when it's his or her turn, each hint-giver draws a song.

The hint-giver then gives clues as to the song's identity. Younger children might keep the hints simple, like "I'm thinking of a song about a girl named Mary who has a wooly pet." Older players can convey the song's plot; for instance, "This song is about a girl whose mischievous pet makes friends with her teacher and classmates." For an added challenge, have the hint-giver describe the plot without using any of the words in the title.

Whoever thinks he or she knows the identity of the tune first gets to sing the song. If the guesser is correct, the hint-giver and the rest of the family can join in. Otherwise, the hint-giver continues to offer clues. This is one game that ought to be music to your ears.

To and Fro

Required:
Paper,
art supplies

A popular song once pointed out that "one man's ceiling is another man's floor." In this drawing game, one person's smile may well be another's eyebrows—with hilarious results!

Two people work together to create this top-to-bottom drawing of a person's face. To start, have the two artists sit facing each other with a sheet of paper between them on an armrest or table. Draw a large oval on the page so that the long dimension runs from one artist to the other, then have children take turns adding facial features.

Because each child's view is upside-down in relation to the other's, the features added will take on a different meaning for each child. If one draws a mouth, for example, it may become frown lines from the other child's perspective. In the same way, eyebrows that one child draws could look like bags under the eyes of the other's face. By the time they have completed their drawing, your children will have created two completely different faces.

To and Fro

Who knows which is right-side up?

High-Flying Scavenger Hunt

Scavenger hunts are always a lot of fun, but it's impossible to have one on an airplane. Or is it?

Required:
In-flight magazines, catalogs

Your children can go on an exciting scavenger hunt without ever leaving their seats simply by using the complimentary airline magazines and in-flight catalogs stowed in the seat-back pocket in front of you.

Scan through the magazine and catalog ahead of time and make a list of scavenger-hunt treasure pictures. Pick photographs that lend themselves to interesting clues. A picture of a pool float in a catalog, for example, could be described as "something to keep your head above water," and the clue for a picture of a sandy beach could be "bring a towel and watch out for sea gulls."

When your kids are ready to go on their scavenger hunt, give them each a copy of the magazine or catalog, along with your list of clues, and send them off to find their treasures.

To and Fro

House Hunting

Looking for a dream house? Why not transact a real estate deal as you make your travels?

One person takes on the role of real estate broker and tries to sell the other passengers on various homes (it doesn't matter whether or not they have For Sale signs). The broker begins by asking the potential buyers what qualities they're most interested in (a giant water slide in the backyard, a horse corral, or perhaps a kitchen with a built-in ice-cream dispenser). He or she then scouts for hot properties along the route, talking up their wondrous features, perhaps even relating a story or two about impressive former occupants ("Did you know that the inventor of the shoelace lived here? She was actually trying to create a new type of spaghetti but let it overcook").

When the buyers are convinced they've found the house they've always wanted, they negotiate a deal with the broker (the tender doesn't have to be cash, either). Then everyone switches roles.

So, how much did you pay for that charming little yellow house with the white porch?

To and Fro

How Long Would It Take?

Here's a creative way to get your child's mind off the ride—and flex his or her math muscles while you're at it.

Ask your child how long he or she thinks the trip would take if your family were walking, running, or bicycling, on horseback, or in a supersonic plane. For example, if you have 100 miles to go, walking (at 2 miles per hour) would take 50 hours to get there (Distance = Rate ÷ Time). Running would be better (12 miles per hour for a world-class marathoner); you'd arrive in 8 hours and 20 minutes. Of course, a horse is faster still (at 25 miles per hour).

Don't forget a cheetah (50 miles per hour), a race car (125 miles per hour), and the Japanese bullet train (250 miles per hour).

If your child is in a real hurry, he or she could travel at the speed of sound (700 miles per hour) and arrive before you could say "Are we there yet?" And for the ultimate trip, traveling at the speed of light (186,000 miles per second) your family would arrive before your child could even think of the question!

To and Fro

In-Flight Map Game Pack

Required:
In-flight magazine, writing supplies

With a little imagination and a pencil, the route map in your complimentary airline magazine can become a whole package of games and puzzles (see activities 62 and 82 for other ideas). Try engaging your child with these games:

Connect the dots. Trace selected route lines to create a picture of an animal, person, or thing.

How NOT to get there. Devise the longest route imaginable to travel from one city to another.

Alphabet tally. Count all the places on the map whose names begin with the same letter.

Multi-city shopping spree. Plan a trip to various places on the map to sample local products (Florida oranges, Wisconsin cheese, Texas oil, New England maple syrup, and so on).

By the way, did you know that the *worst* way to get from Bali to Oslo is by way of Yap, Chuuk, Tegucigalpa, and Cleveland?

To and Fro

In-Flight Route Talks

The route map in your complimentary airline magazine can be a great starting point for all kinds of discussions. Try these topics for starters:

Required:
In-flight magazine

Places you have been. Tell your child about places on the map where you have traveled or lived. Fill him or her in on the climate, any unusual land features, and so on.

What do you know? Engage your child in a conversation about what he or she knows about various places on the map. What do the countries produce? What language do the inhabitants speak? What sorts of foods are eaten there?

Distances. Use examples (such as the distance to the city where Grandma lives) to give your child some perspective about how far different places on the map are from home.

Don't be surprised if, after the first map discussion, you and your child are off on your own imaginary journey!

To and Fro

83 Land Ho!

If your family is spending any time on a ferry or a cruise ship, and your kids don't want to sit still, maybe they'll enjoy performing an "official duty."

Keep watch with your kids, and have them record their observations about the sea at regular intervals. As they make their "sightings" ask about what they see. For example:

Sea gulls. Can your kids keep track of how many are around the ship?

Horizon. Have your kids note what's visible in different directions at any given time, and talk about how things appear over the horizon.

Sighting chart. As you approach land, have your kids pick a tall landmark like a church steeple and "measure" it by sighting along a pencil held at arm's length. They can mark a line on a piece of paper to represent each sighting.

After a little time on board, your kids will become knowledgeable old salts when it comes to shipboard travel.

To and Fro

Layover Games

Have you ever found yourself stuck at an airport with your children with plenty of time to get bored but not quite enough time to go off and do something? If so, you'll appreciate these easy games!

Alphabet scavenger hunt. Walk around the terminal with your kids and have them find objects that begin with every letter in the alphabet. Start them off with, naturally, *A* for airplane.

Guess the destination. Before you reach a gate, have everyone guess where the plane parked at that jetway will be going.

Who's up next? Watch the planes taking off and keep tabs on which airline has the most flights, or have your kids guess which airline will take off next.

Carousel races. Take a position near a luggage carousel and have your kids try to pick which of the people standing there will be the first to get their suitcases.

Now departing from all gates, flight 3210, takeoff for fun!

To and Fro

85 License Plate Scrabble

Required:
Writing supplies

Kids always like to check out the license plates on the highway to see where the cars are from. Here's a new license-plate game your children can play that is especially well suited to young readers.

Give each child paper and a pencil and have him or her write down letters from the license plates of passing cars. Decide ahead of time how many cars your kids can use to "stockpile" letters. When that number is reached, allow a fixed amount of time to see how many words each child can make using the letters he or she has accumulated. If you want to score the game, give two points for two-letter words, three for three-letter words, and so on.

As a variation, have your kids see how many cars they need to spot to find all the letters in their name or a portion of it. You can also vary these games by including letters from billboards and road signs.

Perhaps you can award a bonus to the first child who can spell "Welcome to Mississippi!"

To and Fro

License to Remember

If your fellow passengers are up to a real challenge—as well as a good time—then why not organize a license plate memory tournament or another memory challenge?

Required:
Writing supplies

The idea of this brain challenge is to try to remember a list of items from license plates on passing cars and trucks. Each player recites the list, then adds another item to it. (Someone can act as referee by writing the list down and checking each participant's recollection.)

Other memory lists might include:

- Car colors
- Signs: Each person adds a sign to the list and recites all the preceding signs
- Number of passengers in the cars
- Farm animals you pass
- Types of trucks

Whoever recites the longest list suggests the category for the next game. Or, perhaps that person becomes the referee.

However you play, by the time you get to your destination, you'll all be memory champions!

To and Fro

List Mania

Do your kids enjoy putting things in categories? Here's a simple list-making game they can play anytime, anywhere.

The game is played by selecting a category and then trying to think of as many things as possible that fit into it. Your children can keep a written list or simply call out answers. The categories can be geared for your child as appropriate:

Animals	Mountains
Song titles	Rocks
Places we have visited	States
Extinct things	Countries of the world
American history	Presidents
Articles of clothing	Rainforest animals
Things in our house	Flowers
Kitchen utensils	Rivers

All of these topics can be made more specific. For example, "animals" could be limited to "animals that climb trees" or "North American mammals"; "things in our house" could be narrowed to "things in our house made of wood," and so on.

Hey, here's one. How about a list of how many wrong turns we've made on this trip?

To and Fro

They say that every person has a look-alike. Perhaps the same holds true for cars, minivans, campers, and the like. Can your child find a vehicle on the road that's a clone of yours?

Ask your child to scrutinize the cars, trucks, vans, and other vehicles that you pass. He or she then finds those that are of the same color as your own. Other find-it possibilities include license plates that contain one or more of the same letters or numbers as yours, vehicles that are of the same make or model, and those that contain the same passenger composition (for example, two grownups and one child).

You might set a time limit for each round. Encourage your child to find more blue cars or license plates that contain a *Y* than he or she did in the previous round. Or challenge your family to a car-search contest: each participant gets a set amount of time to find cars matching a predetermined list of characteristics (color, number of passengers, etc.), and then see who comes up with the most lookalikes.

Did anyone spot a gray station wagon with two grownups, two kids, and a couple of cats? That's us!

To and Fro

Log Those Plates!

Required:

Writing
supplies,
notebook

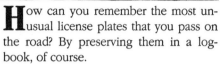

How can you remember the most un-usual license plates that you pass on the road? By preserving them in a log-book, of course.

To make a log, use a notebook or sheets of paper that can later be stapled together. At the top of each page write the time span of each license-watch period (say 8:15 to 8:30 AM) and the watch cate-gory (in this case, out-of-state license plates).

You and your co-travelers scout the road and look for out-of-state license plates. The designated log keeper (you or an older child) then makes a list of the li-cense plates as they are spotted.

Your family can also watch for and log other license-plate features, including col-ors, slogans, and letters and digits (for ex-ample, how many license plates can you find that contain the letter *W*?).

You can reserve a special section in your logbook for vanity plates. See who can find the funniest, most original, or most cryptic in a given time period. Then log the ultimate challenge: the number of license plates each family member can memorize in one sitting.

To and Fro

Logos to Go!

Whether or not you pass billboards during your travels, you're sure to be deluged with advertising.

See how creative your children can be as they design their own travel-related logos, trademarks, symbols, and tag lines for vacation stops, shops, restaurants, cars, gas stations, houses, buildings, mountains, rivers, lakes, and other objects that you pass.

The logos your children devise can be serious, communicating their opinions and perceptions, or silly. An airline logo might depict an eagle with the caption "Fly with us" or "Never-on-time airlines." A train might sport a picture of a train crossing a steep mountain and the slogan, "We know we can, we know we can, we know we can. . . ." For a hotel chain, how about a pair of big feet on a fluffy globe with the tag line, "The best place in the world to rest your weary feet." Finally, try this one for the family car: A smiling face on the bumper and the slogan, "Mom-mobile gets you there!"

This is clearly a case where advertising pays off—in the form of a fun travel pastime!

To and Fro

Magazine Matching

Required:

Magazines,
Writing supplies

A re you and your traveling companions magazine buffs? Then why not turn an in-flight or train magazine into an opportunity for fun?

First, make a list of pictures and article topics you might expect to find in courtesy magazines: rental cars, computers, hotels, and the like. (If you plan to play along, then no peeking at the magazine cover or flipping through the pages in advance!) One person can keep track of the master list, crossing off items as they're spotted in the magazine.

To up the challenge, magazine matchers can compose a "taboo" list, writing down a predetermined number of pictures and topics they expect *not* to find in the magazine. Players then must deduct one match for every taboo match found.

The winner (whoever chalks up the most matches) gets to create the next list, which you can use to play the matching game with a new magazine. You can reuse the taboo list from the last round or create a new one. It's probably safe to assume that you won't find an article about the rabbit-eared bandicoot in the next magazine, either!

To and Fro

Magazine Memory Circle

Perhaps you can't commit a whole magazine to memory, but you can certainly pretend that you have.

Have participants study the table of contents in an in-flight or other magazine (you might want to limit each traveler's reading time to, say, three minutes). Then put the magazine aside and establish a "memory circle." Decide who will be first, who will be second, and so on, as you play the game.

The first player offers an article title (you should decide in advance whether it has to be the exact title or describing the content of the article is enough). If the player can't remember an actual article, he or she can bluff by inventing an article that really isn't in the magazine. Other players then guess whether the article title is real or made-up. The second player then offers an article title (actual or invented), then the third player, and so on.

See how long you can keep the "memory circle" going. You might find that some of the real articles are stranger than the ones you invent!

Required:
Magazines

To and Fro

93 Makes and Models

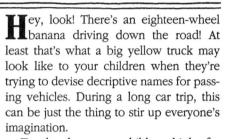

Hey, look! There's an eighteen-wheel banana driving down the road! At least that's what a big yellow truck may look like to your children when they're trying to devise decriptive names for passing vehicles. During a long car trip, this can be just the thing to stir up everyone's imagination.

To play, have your children think of a one- or two-word description for various cars, trucks, and buses they see on the highway. The closer the description matches the vehicle (in shape, color, size, and so on) the better. Of course, humor counts, too, like *"Bar-o-Soap"* for a modern passenger sedan that takes aerodynamic styling to the limit, *"flamingo"* for a construction crane, or *"fido"*—a tow truck with big headlights (eyes), two side mirrors (ears), and a towing hook (tail).

Guess what? The kids in the big red barn (wood-paneled station wagon) are waving at us!

Map Mavens

If your older children are fascinated by maps, here's a way to put that curiosity to good use.

Provide each child with his or her own map of the areas you'll be traveling through, as well as a list of highways you'll be taking. Ask your kids to trace your trip, and see if they can figure out where you are. They can also use the bar scale in the map legend or the mileage indicated for different sections of the road to figure out how much farther you have to go. Combine that bit of information with a little math (see activity 57), and your kids won't have to ask, "When are we going to get there?" They'll be able to figure it out themselves.

You may also want to give some clues regarding the most recently passed exit or town. How can you tell where you are at any given moment? Are there any signs around that give an indication? Perhaps the road itself has mile markers.

Who knows? Next time, your young navigators may propose an entirely different route. You might even cut your travel time in half!

Required:
Road maps

To and Fro

Matching Postcards

Required:
Paper,
art supplies

Can your family predict what pictures you'll find on postcards during your travels?

Participants draw a specific number of pictures of scences that they anticipate they'll find on postcards at the next stop. Later, at a rest stop or other place that sells postcards, they see how many actually match.

For a greater challenge, assign a point value to each picture in advance. For instance, each passenger's first drawing might be worth one point, his or her second drawing two points, and so on. Or you might assign points based on the chances of finding a postcard with a matching drawing (for example, the Empire State Building might be worth one point, while Grand Central station might count for three). Then, at the next stop, see who collects the most points by matching pictures.

You might also include some tricky rules: if his or her picture appears on more than three postcards, the drawer has to subtract three points. That should discourage travelers from clamoring to draw the Golden Gate Bridge!

To and Fro

Mixed-Up Seasons

How would you like to turn your summer vacation into a spring break (or a winter or autumn respite)? Here's how.

Required:
Paper,
art supplies

First, have your children draw a scene as they see it out the window. For example, if it's summer in Vermont, your children might draw rows of green-leafed trees. Now ask your kids to imagine that it's winter, and have them create new drawings of the scene, adding snow and holiday lights to the trees. Then they can draw the same scene in the spring and in the autumn.

As a variation, ask your children to imagine they're driving through the tropics and suddenly it begins to snow. Have them draw "before" and "after" pictures, or write (or tell) a story about what happens. Your kids can also draw and write tales about other incongruous places and season changes (the North Pole during a heat wave, the desert in the midst of a freak ice storm).

You might learn that cactus plants turn remarkable colors after a major snowfall!

To and Fro

More Map Games

Required:
Map,
paper,
writing supplies

$\mathbf{M}$ap games are perfect for long car trips. Try these while you make your way toward your first destination.

Hot and cold. Provide a copy of a map and announce that you are trying to get to a certain place. Give a clue, like the first letter of the destination. Your child then gives descriptions like "I'm going west on I-80," to which you reply "hot" if that will lead to the secret destination or "cold" if it leads away.

Map hangman. Select a place on the map and have your kids guess which letters are in the name. If a player guesses a letter correctly, write that letter down on a piece of paper in its appropriate position. If a player guesses an incorrect letter, draw a part of a stick figure. Your kids have to guess all of the letters (or say the name of the place) before the figure is complete. Once they guess the name have them find it on the map.

Now for the greatest challenge: See if any of your kids can refold the map so it fits back in the glove compartment!

To and Fro

More Word Games

When your family is cruising along, passing sign after sign and billboard after billboard, why not use the words to have some fun? Here are some interesting word-game ideas (for other word games, see activities 65 and 70):

Required:
Writing supplies

Word finder: Allow a fixed amount of time (or miles) for everyone to select a word from a sign or billboard and write it on a piece of paper. Then see how many new words each player can make by rearranging the letters.

Place phrases: Using only place names from signs, see what phrases everyone can come up with, silly or sensible. Each phrase must have at least four words.

Riddles and limericks: Using place names on signs, try to make up riddles and limericks. For example:

> There once was a fellow from L.A.
> Who loved to go outside and play.
> But he fell off his swing,
> And hurt his left wing,
> And now he just sits home all day!

To and Fro

99 Name Games

Traveling provides a great opportunity for collecting interesting names. Passengers can compile lists of stores and restaurants with offbeat monikers and then try the following:

Stores of strangeness. Develop zany inventory lists. For example, the Exotic Pet Palace might sell talking lizards, walking snakes, six-legged parakeets, and human-sized goldfish.

Menu madness. Design a menu for odd-sounding eating establishments. The Rain Forest Cafe, for instance, might serve Evergreen Salads, Maple Sap Soda, Acorn Chips, and Berry Burgers.

Customer profiles. Describe the store's or restaurant's possible patrons. Perhaps there's a landscaper who shops the Exotic Pet Palace for interesting creatures to add to his clients' lawns and gardens.

Compare your view of what goes on behind the signs with your children's perceptions. Who knows? Perhaps everything you need to know about an establishment is in its name!

To and Fro

Name That Tape

Here's a road version of Name That Tune. Before the trip, your child or another family member tapes some songs. Be sure to include tunes that the whole family is familiar with (as a special surprise, you might even want to tape each person's favorite song).

Required:
Tape recorder

Once you're on the road, designate an emcee to work the tape recorder. He or she says "now" and plays several notes of the first song on the tape. Listeners take turns guessing the name of the melody. The emcee then plays several more notes to verify which, if any, of the guesses are correct. The emcee can continue playing portions of the song until everyone recognizes the song. He or she can then play the rest of the tune (your family can sing along) before the game begins again. Whoever guesses the song correctly gets to emcee the next song.

Doesn't time fly when you're listening to your favorite tunes?

To and Fro

Required:

Laundry marker,
shoebox,
paper tags with
strings,
wax paper,
notebook
writing supplies

I t's fun collecting souvenirs during family trips, but wouldn't you like to encourage your children to find keepsakes other than the typical trinkets that get broken or lost before you get home? For some vacations, especially car trips with plenty of stops at parks and other natural attractions, a traveling nature collection may be just the way for your kids to commemorate their journey.

Anything goes for this souvenir collection, including rocks, pine cones, and twigs. Help your children gather and organize their treasures, and label each with a date and place.

Rocks can be labeled with a laundry marker and kept in a shoebox, while paper tags with strings are perfect for labeling pine cones and twigs.

Pressed leaves can also make great souvenirs. Have your children press the leaves in a notebook between pieces of wax paper, then add written notes about when and where the leaves were found.

To and Fro

When your children get home, not only will they enjoy having added to their nature collection, but they'll be reminded of the fun they had putting it all together.

Nautical Careers

If your older kids are enjoying their ocean travels, perhaps they should consider a nautical career.

Before your children commit to specific ship-related occupations, they can interview various crew members and others who work on the ship—maybe even the captain—and learn what they do, what they like best about their job, the best places they've sailed to, etc. (Often people who work on ships are amenable to taking a few minutes to talk to children, but be sure your kids check in advance to see whether they've caught the potential interviewee at a convenient time.)

Your children can then transcribe the important points of each interview into an "Aboard-Ship Careers" notebook. Later, your children can fill you in on which career he or she has chosen and the reasons why it's appealing. You can choose a career that sounds tempting, as well. Your career choices need be limited only by your imagination. Who says the cruiseship industry doesn't have room for five more captains?

Required:
Notebook, writing supplies

To and Fro

Navigator's Hat

Required:
Hat,
map, markers

Even if your children aren't old enough to drive, they can still help get you to your destination. Make (or select) a special hat before you leave home. Then have your kids take turns wearing the hat and perform the following navigator duties:

Sign spotter. If you're looking for a particular town or exit, or the next rest area, have the navigator watch for signs.

Map travel recorder. The navigator traces your route on a map with a highlighter pen, adding markers in the appropriate places to indicate all of your stops.

Travel updater. Have your navigator periodically report which direction you're heading in, how far you've gone, and how many miles you have to travel until the next stop.

And, of course, when you come to a crossroads and don't have a clue as to where you are, the navigator can help you guess which way to go next!

To and Fro

Odometer Olympics

Who says you can't hold the Olympics in the backseat of your car? All you need is an odometer!

The driver of the car gives the signal when the odometer reaches a good starting point ("Ready, get set, go!"), then stops the event after a predetermined distance. Try these events to get started:

Clapoff. Have your children clap their hands as many times as possible in the allotted distance. (Keep it short if the driver will find it distracting.)

Numberathon. See who can count the highest in the given time.

Finger exercises. How many times can your children flex their fingers in the given amount of miles?

Heads, shoulders, knees. Have your children touch their own heads, shoulders, and knees as many times as possible in the time span.

By the way, since you're in the car, you can skip the torch-lighting ceremony.

To and Fro

To and Fro

Here's a game that will test your family's memory as well as their powers of imagination.

The first player says, "I see an island, and on that island is . . ." and fills in an object—for instance, "a purple pineapple tree." The second player repeats, "I see an island, and on that island is a purple pineapple tree" and then adds something of his or her own—for example, "a seven-foot-tall pirate." The next player repeats the sentence with the previous items, adds something of his or her own, and so on. See who can remember the longest list and who can contribute the silliest items.

An alternative way to play, especially for older children, is to have all of the items relate to one theme—say, a tropical storm. The list might then include "yellow rain, sky-splitting thunder, falling blue coconuts, a tent with a leak in it," and so on. When the game is finished, players can tell a story that incorporates all of the items from the memory list. Younger kids can draw a picture of what happens on the imaginary island.

Those coconuts must have been quite a sight!

Palindromes

Palindromes are words or phrases that read the same backward and forward. Some palindromes are both complicated and silly (for instance, "Able was I ere I saw Elba," or "A man, a plan, a canal, Panama!") There are also plenty of simple words young children can spell that are palindromes.

Have your kids think of as many palindromic words as possible. Some they are likely to know are "mom," "pop," "dad," "tot," "toot," and "noon." Your children can also include names, like Anna, Hannah, and Bob.

As your kids think of palindromes, they can incorporate them into a story (weaving them together with non-palindromes so that the plot makes sense). Try this tale, which begins with two classic palindromes, for starters: "Madam, I'm Adam. Was it a cat I saw? Mom called at noon. She wanted to find dad so they could pop over to the tot lot and toot their horn."

Wow!

To and Fro

Pass the Exits

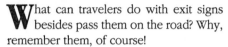

What can travelers do with exit signs besides pass them on the road? Why, remember them, of course!

Appoint a passenger to read and write down exit signs, including names and numbers, as they appear. (This works best with a series of exit signs in close proximity.) Players see whether they can remember and recite the signs—in reverse order.

For example, let's say you've passed three signs. The first player recites the list from memory (for example, "exit 16, Wilson City; exit 15, Clearfield; exit 14, Riverdale"). After passing the next sign, the second player adds, "exit 17, South Sunset," and then recites the other three signs. The next player adds the new sign and recites the other four, and so on, until players can no longer remember the whole list.

Map readers can try this variation. One person identifies the next three exits on the map. Players then memorize the exit names and numbers, and try to recall them *before* the exit sign appears. That's one great way to put your astounding memory on the map!

To and Fro

Patterns

Does your child like making and finding patterns? If so, he or she will enjoy this pattern puzzle. It's easy to do, and the results are never the same twice.

Required:
Art supplies

Begin the puzzle by drawing a series of simple geometrical shapes on a sheet of paper to create a repetitive pattern. The more shapes you use, the more complicated the pattern can become. It can be as simple as

●■|●■|●■|

or something more elaborate, like

●●■△■■|■●●■△■■|■

Now see if your child can figure out the pattern and continue it. For a more challenging puzzle, you and your child can create a two-dimensional pattern, such as

After a while, you and your child will certainly notice another pattern developing: that time flies when you're having fun!

To and Fro

Pennants and Flags

Required:
Art supplies

W hat's special about the cities or states you're traveling through? Here's an opportunity for your kids to show you.

Have your young artists draw a custom pennant or flag for each place you pass.

The pennant or flag should contain the name of the city or state, and the design should say something about the place: big, bold letters might be appropriate for a booming metropolis, while small letters might bespeak a rustic community. Your children can also add pictures, symbols, or designs that give the flavor of the place.

And, of course, your pennant and flag designers will want to include slogans. For example:

Texas. Oil we want is to make you welcome!

New York. Bigger and more fun than Old York.

Boston. More than just a hill of beans.

Florida. The place to be in Januareee!

When you get back home, your children can use their pennants and flags to decorate their rooms and commemorate their travels.

To and Fro

Personalized Postcards

How would you and your co-travelers like to pose for postcard pictures?

Passengers choose a postcard, either bought or created on the way, with an interesting scene. Then participants make a drawing of a fellow passenger, or perhaps a self-portrait on a separate piece of paper, and affix it to the postcard. Or instead of sketching additional people, artists can add a drawing of your home or another local landmark, such as their school, a monument, or a bridge.

Required:
Postcards,
tape/glue,
art supplies,
paper

If the original postcard is already full, simply cut out a pictured object or two, such as one building on a block or two people in a crowd. Then paste or tape a trimmed sheet of paper to the back of the postcard, and add personalized drawings that show through the hole.

Once the postcard is revised, passengers write a message. (Remember to mail it in an envelope when you have the opportunity.) Won't your friends back home be surprised to see a picture of your children standing in the doorway of the White House?

To and Fro

111 Picture Playtime

Required:

Traveling Picture Kit (see activity 20)

If you've made a Traveling Picture Kit (activity 20), then you have what it takes to instantly entertain all the members of your family. Try these for starters:

Auction. Select several pictures from the picture bag and auction them off. Give each child an imaginary one hundred dollars. The auctioneer tries to sell each object by describing its artistic merits.

Guess the picture. One person chooses a picture and gives other passengers clues about its identity. Whoever guesses correctly gets to pick the next picture.

Take and match. Pass the bag around and have each of your children take a picture from it. Then see if everyone can match his or her picture to something he or she actually saw on the road.

Your children can supplement the picture-kit photos by adding their own drawings, as needed. Isn't it amazing how anyone can draw Snoopy when he or she really needs to?

To and Fro

Puppet Road Shows

If you've made Puppets to Go (activity 25), here are some ideas for performing the best, plays on the road:

Coming soon. Your puppets can rehearse some real-life travel adventures (getting to the hotel, dining with grandparents, touring an amusement park, exploring a zoo). Simply check your agenda, share it with your fellow puppeteers, and rehearse the vacation activities still to come.

Tour guides. Maybe you don't have friends or relatives who can show you around in each of the cities and towns that you pass, but you surely know some puppets who will take you on a tour. Let the puppets show you the sights as only long-time residents can.

Travel recaps. How much of your vacation fun can you recall at the end of each day? Puppets can act out the highlights of your adventures and help everyone commit your traveling activities to memory.

Once you and your fellow puppeteers begin, you're sure to discover a trip's worth of great puppet drama!

Required:
Puppets to Go
(see activity 25)

To and Fro

113

Reporter at Large

Required:

Notebook, writing supplies/tape recorder

Here's a neat way to pass some time at the gate before you take off.

For interviewing equipment, use either a notebook and pen or a tape recorder. Choose an older child or an adult to be the story assignment editor. Then brainstorm about potential interviewees: other passengers, gate attendants (if they're not too busy), flight attendants waiting to board, food vendors, etc. Next, have the editor assign a team of reporters to conduct each interview. You might want to pair up older and younger children; in any case, be nearby during the interview.) It's a good idea to have your kids keep it brief.

Sample interview questions include: Where are you going? Have you been there before? Do you travel often? Do you like to travel? Where would you most like to be traveling today?

Preserve the interview notes or tapes, and have reporters turn the most interesting ones into feature stories.

So the three-year-old boy in the next seat said that he was going to visit his grandmother's pet lion, did he?

To and Fro

Right and Left Drawings

What do you see out the window? That depends upon which side of the car or train you're sitting on.

Find out what your fellow travelers are seeing and how their window views compare with yours by drawing the sights. Each participant gets some drawing paper, crayons, markers, and other art supplies. When you say, "Now," each person draws what he or she sees while looking out the right or left window. (Those sitting in the middle should choose one view and stick to it for the duration of the activity.)

Give the cue to draw at various intervals (say, every half-hour or so). Artists should write the time when they begin drawing on the bottom of each picture (older children can help younger siblings). When each person has amassed a pile of drawings, arrange the pictures in chronological order, with the first one at the top. The artists then trade and compare pictures.

So what were your left-seat counterparts seeing while you watched a cow grazing in the meadow? A group of tourists taking pictures of Rockefeller Center? Fascinating!

Required:
Art supplies

To and Fro

Right and Left Guess-It

🚗 🚂 ✈

As you discovered in the previous activity, where you sit greatly colors what you see. Here's a right/left guessing game that will entertain all your passengers, regardless of where they're sitting.

The game involves a right team and a left team. People sitting in the middle should choose a side in advance and stick to it for the duration of the game.

The right team chooses a spokesperson, who then spies something interesting out the window (say, a red barn) and whispers to other team members what the object is. The left-team players take turns asking yes-or-no questions (right-team members also take turns answering). After each turn, a left-team member can guess the object's identity. When somebody guesses it correctly, the left team chooses a spokesperson, and the game begins again.

During the game, passengers also might want to log the items seen from the right and left windows. Otherwise, who would believe that the right team was looking at a barn while the left team was spying a skyscraper!

Road Matches

Required:
Homemade cards

A re your younger kids looking for a great way to play with their home-made Deck the Road cards (see activity 26)? Then try this traveling card game (older kids might help with the scoring).

Each player gets five cards. Participants are free to look at other players' cards as well. Players watch the road (other players can join in the search) and try to find any of the objects pictured on their cards (for instance, a red stop sign or a yellow truck).

If the matching object is also of a matching color, the player earns two points, puts the card at the bottom of the deck, and picks a new card. If the object is right but the color is wrong, the player gets one point and returns the card to the deck, drawing a fresh one. Then it's the next player's turn.

The game ends when all players have earned ten points (or however many points you establish in advance). Then start over again to play a new game.

Would you like to try a bit of match-making?

To and Fro

Road Math

If your kids' restlessness and irritability seem to be multiplying with the miles, try this arithmetic game for a brain-bending diversion.

The game can be played individually or in teams. For the basic version, have your children add any numbers they spot on highway signs, and see if they can reach a target value—say, 100. As your children get going with the game, you can make it a little more complicated by adding rules such as: Add the numbers you see on the right side of the road, but subtract those that you see on the left.

For kids who are more advanced at math, try this challenge. Pick a target number and have them use any numbers they see to add, subtract, multiply, or divide and hit the target exactly.

Whatever you do, you're sure to find that CAR + KIDS - BOREDOM X MILES = FUN!

Roadside Charades

Charades on the go—what a way to while away the miles!

Look out the window, and when you see something interesting (for example, a crane working on a new building), act it out, (be sure not to distract the driver), and see if co-travelers can guess the object. To up the challenge, guessers can close their eyes while you look out the window.

Alternatively, play a game of charades that involves the area you're traveling through. Children can study the map ahead of time for inspiration, or you can simply improvise as you travel. When you reach a river, bridge, mountain, or the like with an interesting name, you and your children act it out. For example, when you pass the Golden Gate bridge, one family member might point to a gold necklace or ring, another player might pretend to open a gate, and a third player might pantomime a game of bridge. The player who comes up with the most original clue gets to choose the next roadside charade.

Okay, now, can any of your co-travelers think of a way to act out the Ompompanoosuc River in Vermont?

To and Fro

Scavenger Hunt at 30,000 Feet

Required:

In-flight magazines, writing supplies

You can always count on airlines to provide you with free reading—and guessing game—materials.

Look through an in-flight magazine (or another publication that a family member has brought along) with your child. Make a list of about ten items for your child to find (don't let him or her see what you're jotting down). For example, you might find a tree, a blue sailboat, a woman with a suitcase, a dog, a man in a suit, an airline pilot, a map, an airplane, and so on.

If you're traveling with more than one child and you only have one copy of the magazine, your kids can work together as a team to find each item. Or, if each child has his or her own copy of the magazine, make separate lists so that your kids can work on the hunt individually.

For an added challenge, put a time limit on the hunting: a set interval of time or a time limit related to an unpredictable event (e.g., the pilot making an announcement).

Oops. Here comes the snack cart now—are your kids ready to hunt down a few peanuts?

To and Fro

Scrabble Plates

Bored with magnetic board games? Then try this road version of Scrabble!

First, players choose seven to ten "tiles" (letters culled from license plates or signs that you pass). Each player keeps track of his or her own tiles on paper. You can then assign point values to each letter; vowels may be worth one point while common consonants merit three points and those like Q and X are worth ten.

Taking turns, passengers form words, using as many of their letters as possible in each turn. Players who use all their letters at once might earn a bonus of, say, five points. And you might offer a double bonus for players who think of two words that use all the letters. Each time a player uses a letter he or she draws another to replace it by choosing a letter on the closest license plate or sign.

As a variation, players can pool all their letters. Family members then take turns making words, choosing new tiles as old ones are used. See who can come up with the longest word, a word that relates to your destination, or even use the tiles to spell a whole sentence.

Required:
Writing supplies

To and Fro

121 Sea Tales

When your family members look out at the deep blue sea, perhaps they're recalling the greatest adventures of their lives. For example:

Goodwill pirate. The pirate in your family can tell about the day he or she was elected the "Goodwill Ambassador Pirate" and promised to turn over a new leaf and spend his or her time doing good deeds.

Sea-monster mash. Have your resident sea monster recount the time he or she threw the biggest birthday party in ocean history, inviting ten thousand of his or her closest sea-monster friends.

Whale watch. If there are any whales in your family, they can tell about going on a "people watch" cruise. Were they lucky enough to spot three human beings?

After the first round of adventure telling, family members can switch roles and weave new tales (or finish stories that other storytellers began). That's the quickest way we know of for a pirate or a sea monster to turn into a whale of a tale!

To and Fro

Are the images rushing past your windows starting to blur? Then take a moment to organize what you're seeing into meaningful sequences, and find out whether other passengers can see them, too.

Take turns calling out sequences involving colors, shapes, heights, numbers, and so on. For example, you might say, "Who sees two blue cars and a yellow car?" or "Who sees two short buildings and a tall building?" Whoever sees the sequence first suggests the next one.

As a variation, passengers can offer a cryptic sequence, such as "Who sees three ice-cream cones?" Other participants take turns guessing what that hint refers to (they might be cloud shapes, symbols on signs, houses with pointed roofs, and so on). Or the sequence-giver might call out a sequence that he or she doesn't yet see (say, four cars followed by a minivan) and look for it right along with the other players.

So who sees a fun-filled vacation followed by a lot of terrific memories?

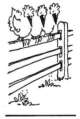

To and Fro

123 Shape Search

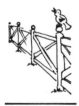

To and Fro

Houses, trees, rivers, bridges, cars, trucks. When your children describe what they see from the window, are these the things on the list? Why not get them to look at their surroundings a little differently—say, in terms of circles, squares, and maybe even a trapezoid or two?

To begin this geometry exercise, make a list of basic shapes and forms. You can include circles, squares, rectangles, triangles, ovals, columns, spheres, pyramids, and cubes. Then, have your children look out the car window and try to find one example of every shape on the list. If your children are older, consider eliminating the obvious answers, like wheels.

As your kids get better at seeing geometrically, have them be on the lookout for new shapes to add to their list. They may even want to keep a tally of each type they spot. You can also encourage them to look for shapes within shapes by dissecting what they see: a double window, for example, that is a rectangle made up of two squares.

Well, this *is* shaping up to be a lot of fun!

"**S**ervices, Food, Lodging—Next Exit 2 Miles." How about using those ho-hum words in a sentence, like "Miles was two hours late for church services the next day because all the food he ate was lodging in his teeth, and he couldn't get it to exit"?

If you get your children started building sentences from words on road signs, trucks, and billboards, they may not want to stop. And you may hear a lot about this guy Miles by the time you get home.

Encourage your kids to let loose with this game, and have everyone in the car try their creativity with whatever sign strikes his or her fancy. If you want to make it more challenging, have players take turns on whatever words they can spot in a fixed amount of time when it's their turn. Anyone who can use all the words on a sign gets a round of applause.

Hey, dad, lets keep right on going to the next exit and get five ice-cream cones for Miles and his friends!

Sign Word Change

Required:
Thesaurus/
synonym
dictionary

"**E**nsuing egress 5,280 feet." You probably won't see this message on any road sign, but you will, no doubt, encounter the more familiar "Next Exit 1 Mile."

It's great fun to make up fancy renditions of road signs, the more outlandish the better, like "Telecommunications, Sustenance, Bivouacking—Outlet VII: for "Phone, Food, Camping—Exit 7."

Older kids will enjoy making word substitutions for road signs, truck signs, or building signs. The goal is to make the sign as zany as possible, while retaining the original meaning. (It's helpful, though not essential, to bring along a small thesaurus or synonym finder for this activity.)

For a variation, you can reverse this game by making up road signs using complicated words and having your children decipher them. Either way, parental units and offspring will relish a surpassingly diverting recreation!

Silence Is Golden

Need some quieter time while you're traveling, or perhaps a challenging game with a different slant? Then try this.

Assign someone the role of "it." That person tries to make another person say something. Depending on the age of the players, this may be relatively easy—perhaps asking a young child a simple yes-or-no question. For older players, it might take some ingenuity: "it" can ask questions nonchalantly like, "Anyone see that thing that just flew in the window?"

If ingenuity doesn't have the desired effect, perhaps some tall tales will. The person who is "it" can simply take advantage of the opportunity to spin endless, pointless yarns without interruption. That's sure to make someone crack!

Alternatively, make the object of the game to get someone to laugh by telling jokes, making funny faces, or asking silly questions. You and your family will probably find it almost impossible to refrain from laughing when the goal is to be serious. Now what's so funny about being on vacation?

To and Fro

Singing in the Rain

Required:
Writing supplies

When is a windshield wiper not a windshield wiper? When it's a metronome!

On a rainy day, when your windshield wipers are tapping out their rhythm (WOOSH, woosh, WOOSH, woosh . . .), your family can listen to the "music" and compose a rap song to fit the beat.

Family members take turns contributing lyrics, line by line. These can relate to your destination, rest stops, towns and cities you're passing through, new friends you've made during your travels, relatives you're going to visit, sights you're going to see, passengers you've spotted on the road, or fellow travelers. Since this is a rap song, there's no melody to memorize, which makes it perfect for younger passengers.

Assign a scribe the task of writing down the words and making copies for each family chorus member. Then the choir can perform. Decide how the group should perform the song: all together, or each family member singing one line at a time.

WOOSH, woosh, WOOSH, woosh . . . now, that's a "rap"!

To and Fro

Smiling Violations

What if your kids patrolled the high-ways and byways looking for drivers who hadn't brushed their teeth before getting behind the wheel? They'd probably have a blast!

Required:
Art supplies, paper

Here's the next best thing, and your kids don't have to unbuckle their seat belts to do it. Just provide art supplies and paper, and suggest that they make up their own tickets listing silly fines and violations, like the following: fine for driving with a cluttered glove compartment—$5,000; sitting in a standing-only zone—$50; parking on top of a bus—pay 17 doughnuts; fine for ruining rain drops with windshield wipers—$3 million.

You can also have your children make up some silly excuses to give to a trooper. "Gee, officer, I'm sorry, but the hamsters in the glove compartment were restless," or "But officer . . . I didn't know I couldn't park my car on the lawn. Then there's always this one: "I'm sorry the car was shaking but we were all just laughing so hard!"

To and Fro

129 Snork!

Here's a great car game that can easily be adjusted to the ages and skills of your children. The point of the game is to have everyone try to guess the identity of an object while one person supplies clues.

To play, one person picks an object that you pass frequently, such as a signpost, a green car, a gas station. Then, each time the car passes a matching object, he or she calls out "snork" (or some other nonsense word). Everyone else tries to figure out what the item is by looking around when they hear the word "snork" and taking a guess.

To increase the challenge, you can make the object very specific. For example, instead of a green car, the person may pick a green car with four people in it that's traveling in the opposite direction. Then, when someone makes a partially correct guess, the chooser can let the guesser know that the answer is close, but not close enough.

The game can also be varied by picking items that come up more or less frequently. But, be careful. If someone picks fence posts, it may all come down to "Snork, snork, snork, snork, snork . . ."

To and Fro

Sounds Like . . .

Onomatopoeia is a term for words that sound like what they are, such as "buzz," "hiss," and "ping." With a little applied theatrics, your kids can probably make a lot of words onomatopoetic.

The word "big," for example, which even though it isn't (big, that is) can certainly sound "big" if said in a deep, resonant voice. And even though "little" is bigger than "big," it won't sound that way if it's said in a soft, squeaky voice.

Make a game out of creating sentences that use words that sound like what they describe, and challenge your kids to use as much tone, volume, and inflection as necessary to take the idea to a silly extreme.

Begin by helping them think of words that genuinely fit the bill: "hiss," "buzz," "crunch," "pop," "sizzle," "bang," and "swish," for example. Then have your children add their own interpretations of how particular words should sound.

So, what's the sound of children pretending to be asleep in the backseat of a car? Snoooore!

To and Fro

Spin Those Discs

Required:

Tape recorder

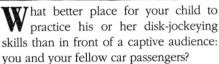

What better place for your child to practice his or her disk-jockeying skills than in front of a captive audience: you and your fellow car passengers?

Before you leave home, you or an older child tapes some favorite tunes of the whole family. Each cassette might have a theme, such as "Broadway Show Classics," "Mom's Favorites," or even "Our Family Sings the Oldies but Goodies." Write down the song titles as they are recorded.

During the trip, your child breaks out the cassette player, identifies himself or herself by a new stage name (such as "The Traveling DJ"), and, referring to the list of songs, introduces the first tune, offering the title and some related trivia—for example, that it's one of the earliest Rodgers and Hammerstein hits. When the song is finished, the DJ announces the next tune.

If the tape includes some instrumentals, the DJ can also sponsor a karaoke contest, with family members taking turns singing while the music plays (rewind the tape after each singer's solo).

Are there any budding on-air personalities in your car?

To and Fro

Start-Stop-Guess

Do your children know how far a mile is? Can they relate that to how fast your car is traveling or how long it takes to get where you're going? Here's a simple car game that will hone your kids' skills for estimating distances.

The object of the game is to guess how far your car has traveled in a given amount of time. When all the players are ready, the driver says "start" and checks the odometer. After a short while, he or she says "stop" and checks the odometer again. Each child then states his or her guess as to how far the car has traveled in the elapsed time.

After you've tried this once or twice, have your children count to themselves from the beginning to the end of a measured mile. Then try the game again with random distances and see if their guesstimates have improved. As a variation, you can have your children take turns issuing the start and stop commands, or have them call out when they think a specified distance has been traveled.

Now when your kids ask, "How far is it?" you can have them take their own best guesses.

To and Fro

This House in History

While you and your family are traveling, why not take a tour of some interesting houses?

Each participant gets a turn to act as tour guide. He or she picks out a house and points it out to fellow passengers. The guide then "walks" family members through the house while explaining the history of the building (from his or her imagination). For example, the guide might say, "Now follow me into the parlor, where in 1786 George Washington enjoyed a cup of tea with the Wilson family."

Tour guides can begin by saying when the house was built. They can then describe each room, pointing out notable furniture, telling when additions to the house were built, and so on. They can also talk about the occupants of the house, prior and current, including the names, where they came from, why they moved into the house, etc.

After the walking tour, family members can question the tour guide about important issues—like the name of the first dog who lived in the house and his favorite form of mischief!

To and Fro

This Stop, Please

If you and your co-travelers can't get off at every train stop and explore, why not at least take some imaginary excursions?

In this activity, your child tells you what your family would see and do if they were getting off at the next stop. If the train stops at a place where your child has been, he or she can describe the trip from memory (including streets, buildings, museums, and restaurants). Otherwise, your child can detail an imaginary route, inventing names of places you might go, people you might meet, and so on.

Alternatively, your child might pretend that the train can stop anywhere in the universe—a distant country, continent, or even planet. He or she can describe the weather, food, houses, and other things that the family will see after stepping off the train. Your child can even create a pretend itinerary detailing the tourist attractions the family will visit (perhaps the Milky Way Planetarium or the Martian Wax Museum).

Next stop, anywhere in the world!

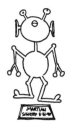

To and Fro

135 This Time Tomorrow

Required:
Writing and art supplies

Here's a way to remind yourself and your fellow passengers that all this traveling is really worth it.

Remind everybody of the next day's itinerary: where you'll be, what you'll do, whom you'll see, and so on. Then, at various intervals during the trip, have your passengers write a paragraph (pre-writers can draw a picture) of what will be happening at the same time tomorrow. For example, if you're planning to arrive at your hotel at four o'clock in the afternoon, participants can write about driving up to the hotel, checking in, settling into their rooms, etc. Then, compare your paragraphs or pictures. Do family members share the same visions of the hotel?

Passengers can also write or draw additional high points of the next day's agenda at appropriate times during your trip. Each time, participants fully imagine and then share their views of what they'll be seeing and doing "this time tomorrow."

Save the writings and pictures. On the return trip, you can see whose visions of your activities most closely matched the real events. Perhaps nobody came close to guessing how great your trip would be!

To and Fro

Town Anthems

Every city or town deserves its own anthem, as well as the right chorus (you and your co-passengers) to sing it.

Required:
Writing supplies

Create a special song based on a familiar melody about an interesting place as you pass through it. The city or town itself can serve as the name of the song. The lyrics can include information about the weather, time of year, and the reason for your trip; the people, buildings, food, and other interesting things you encounter; and what each family member likes best about the place.

Family members can take turns creating the lyrics. You begin by composing a line or two, and then each participant can take a turn and add to the song. Encourage composers to include rhyming couplets, and see whose are the most original or the funniest. You or another designated traveler can write down the lyrics so that you'll have a permanent record of the song.

Once you get back home, your family can use the "sheet music" to sing each of the town anthems that you composed on the road. Isn't it great to have a soundtrack of your trip?

To and Fro

Town Stories

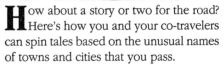

How about a story or two for the road? Here's how you and your co-travelers can spin tales based on the unusual names of towns and cities that you pass.

A designated story starter spies an appropriate sign on the way (for example, "Welcome to Peabody") and reads it aloud. The sign becomes the title of the story. He or she then begins a tale about how the place got its name (for example: Once upon a time there was a king and a queen who had a green dog the size of a pea pod. Naturally, they named him "Peabody."). The story starter can continue the narrative, giving details about how the town was founded, who the original settlers were, what kind of houses they lived in, what types of food they ate, etc., until the story reaches a conclusion.

Alternatively, the story starter can pause at an exciting point in the tale, and another passenger can continue the story, stopping at another cliffhanger for the next person.

You'll undoubtedly be surprised to learn that Peabody the royal dog turned into a human, and then went on to found the first democratic town government!

To and Fro

Trained Guesses

A train trip is a nice change from car travel for your family; there's always lots to see and plenty going on close at hand. Why not play this game to get your kids guessing about the trip and observing more at the same time?

Required:
Writing supplies

To play, you ask your children questions relating to the trip, and they try to guess the answers. Then have everyone watch for the right answer. After a few questions and guesses, your kids will probably want to ask questions, too. Here are some sample questions:

- How long until the next station?
- How many cars will be waiting at the next crossing?
- How soon until another train passes going the other way?
- How many minutes before the conductor comes back into this car?

If you have older children, put them in charge of writing down the questions and guesses. And look for opportunities to ask your children more questions about their guesses. Before you know it, they'll be experts at rail travel!

To and Fro

Travel Collage

Required:
Large sheet of paper,
art supplies

Wouldn't it be convenient to have a "getting there" and "getting home" picture record, all on one sheet of paper. All your child will need are art supplies and a piece of paper—the largest that can be conveniently used while en route.

Have your child look out the window and find something interesting: an unusual house or building or car, a cloud formation that looks like an animal, or a mountain, beach, lake, or pasture. He or she then draws it in on one small area of the paper. When the scenery changes, your child adds another drawing near the first one. So the travel collage might start off showing your city or town, change to rural or farm country, then gradually show a city rising on the horizon, and culminate with a bustling downtown area.

If several artists have created collages, when you get home, you can tape the pieces of paper together and create a wall display. Now *that* will really capture the trip in a way no camera could ever do!

Travel Tally

If your children are entertained by counting things along the highway or rail tracks but are bored with the usual categories of trucks, buses, and license plates from home, try this twist for some variety.

Required:
Writing supplies

To get your children started, give them some unusual categories of things they can count, and have them keep a tally on a piece of paper. You might include silly categories, such as cars driven by men with mustaches, or elaborate ones, like trucks with red lettering going downhill.

You might also try having your children tally items by color, by size ("smaller than the car," "bigger than the car," or "bigger than a truck."), or by building type, (count restaurants, gas stations, office buildings, etc.).

Depending on the region you're passing through, you may want to limit the viewing area so your children can keep up with the tally. But remember, accuracy doesn't count nearly as much as fun!

To and Fro

Traveler's Treasure Hunt

Required:
Writing supplies

Wouldn't it be great if you and your co-travelers could find some hidden treasures?

Make a list of "treasures" you know you'll be passing on your journey: expansion bridges, parks, and so on. If you've taken the route before, you can be specific, listing the name of a restaurant or a hotel. Otherwise, you can note general items, such as "a tall building in Chicago" or "a farm on Interstate 93." Give each participant a copy of the list. Older treasure seekers can check off found objects and help younger players to do the same.

You can plan long-term treasure hunts that will take the whole journey to complete (the final object on the list might be "grandma's house" or "the sign outside your hotel"). Or you can plan a series of treasure hunts using the same list, with such items as "the next exit sign," "the first restaurant we come to," and "a rest stop."

Here's hoping that you won't have to use your treasure-hunting skills to find your child's favorite baseball cap along the way!

To and Fro

Traveling Board Games

W hen the miles get monotonous, pull out the Card-Game Board (activity 24) you made before you left home, and pass the time with some new twists on old favorites.

Required:
Game board
(activity 24)

Highway lotto. Fill the game board pockets with cards placed face up. Every time someone spots something outside the window that matches the image on one of the cards, remove that card. The object of the game is to remove all of the cards in a specified amount of time or by a specified distance.

Highway bingo. To start the game, place the cards in the pockets face up. Every time one of the objects is spotted, turn that card over. Players try to get a complete row or column in the shortest time possible, then call "bingo!" (or a term of your own choosing).

While you've got the game board out, see if your kids can invent their own games. When you get back home, you might even be able market them and pay for a few future vacations.

To and Fro

Traveling Notes

Required:
Writing supplies

Passing notes may not be tolerated in class, but in a car, plane, boat, or train it can be a fun way to pass the time.

Your children can write notes to you, each other, imaginary friends, or famous people they'd like to meet along the way. Here are some starter ideas:

Fortune cookies. "You will take a long car journey to mysterious places."

Travel alerts. "Watch for Falling Bananas" or "Caution: Giant Cicada Crossing Ahead."

Greeting cards. "Congratulations on passing mile marker 156 without a rest stop."

Notes to famous people. "Dear President Lincoln, Why are you hanging out on that mountain with those other three guys?"

Just plain silly. "Don't look now, but there's a slice of apple pie on your head."

Your children can address the notes to other family members, or you can put them in a paper bag and one person can read them aloud.

Here's a note you may well see: "Dad, let's stop for ice cream at the next exit!"

To and Fro

Traveling Shuffle Story

Your family has been driving for three hours, and you still have 150 miles to cover today. Or perhaps the ferry's been out at sea for a bit longer than your kids' patience can tolerate.

Required:

Photos from magazines or catalogs

For this activity, you'll need pictures from magazines and catalogs. Shuffle the pictures and give one of your children the top picture from the stack. Then have him or her use the subject of the picture, along with something he or she can spot in the horizon or along the highway, to make up a story. If the first picture features a dog, for example, and you are driving past a shopping center, the story might begin, "One day, Dorothy the dog went to the supermarket to buy some bananas." Then give the second picture to the next player and have him or her continue the story: "Along the way, she had to stop at the tollbooth and threw her toothbrush in. . . ."

Hopefully, your story won't go to the dogs!

To and Fro

Traveling Word Swap

Required:

Copy of favorite storybook text, writing supplies

When you're traveling, familiar things can often take on a new look. Your children's favorite storybook certainly will if you try this storytelling twist.

Before you head out on your trip, select a few of your children's favorite picture storybooks that have short text. Copy the text, and when you need entertainment announce, "We're going to create a new story!" Don't tell your kids the title of the book. Then page through your copies of the text and find words to replace. (Common nouns or action verbs work best).

For each replacement, ask your children for a word in a particular category—a thing, an animal, an item object, or an action—and have them name something they can spot from the car or train window. Write the replacement word in your copy of the text. When you've gone all the way through the story, read it aloud and be ready for the laughs!

And so, with apologies to Margaret Wise Brown, "In the great green room there was a cement mixer, and a red guardrail and a picture of the cow jumping over the police car. . . ."

To and Fro

Tunnel Vision

The changing world outside the window of a car or train provides a lot of things for your child to look at. This activity will enable him or her to get a different view of the scenery.

To play, all your child needs is a rolled-up piece of paper or a cardboard paper-towel or toilet-paper tube. Your child places the tube up to one eye, closes the other, and watches the passing scenery for a short amount of time (one minute is plenty). Then the child describes what he or she saw in as much detail as possible, based on the view through the tube. You might need to ask some questions to get the descriptions rolling, such as, "Did you see the red house?" You can also ask questions about things that weren't there—like a brown cow—and listen to the detailed descriptions of the phantom animal!

As a variation, have your child provide a running commentary as he or she watches the passing scenery through the tube. You can also vary the game by limiting how much the tube can be moved around. It will be a fun challenge for your child to describe unfamiliar territory from a decidedly narrow view.

Required:
Cardboard tube/rolled-up paper

To and Fro

Under, Over, Around, and Through

Here's a memory game that your family can play while traveling in any kind of vehicle, because the vehicle itself becomes part of the game.

Begin by saying, "The car (or train or plane or boat) went. . . ." Then have your children string together prepositional phrases. For instance, your child might say, "The car went through the mud." The next player repeats the sentence and adds a new phrase, such as "under the bridge." Each child in turn repeats the previous sentences and adds a phrase of his or her own.

If your kids are describing the car, they might end up with something like this:

The car went under a trestle, through a tunnel, over a bridge, around a curve, past a mountain, across a line, beneath a cloud, into a tollbooth, up a ramp, down a hill, out of town . . .

Keep going until the string gets too long to remember. The sentence about the car could conclude, "and finally to Grandma's house!"

Vanity Plates

Vanity, thy name is license plates—if they're custom designed by you and your fellow travelers.

Put your co-passengers to work creating vanity plates for cars, trucks, buses, bicycles, and other vehicles that you pass on the road. The plate might relate to the model or make of the vehicle, weather conditions, where you are, and so on. For example, "2COOL" might be the perfect plate for a convertible, especially if it's a windy day. And "PREZ" might be an appropriate license plate for an important-looking car you pass in Washington, D.C.

Required:
Art supplies

See whether family members can reach a consensus on the ideal vanity plate for each vehicle, or you can "attach" several plates to the same vehicle. Then, the vanity-plate creator draws a picture of the vehicle with its new vanity plate.

Alternatively, you can list vanity-plate slogans beforehand, either on the road or before leaving home, and search for a vehicle that's worthy of bearing each plate. How long will it take to spot a car that you can designate "NO1AUTO"?

To and Fro

Video Trip Record: We're on Our Way!

Required:
Video camera

Bringing out the video camera when you're traveling will not only relieve the boredom of a long drive or ride, but it will provide you with some unusual video memories of the journey. Be sure to include the little things as well as the big events. For instance:

On the road. Give each family member a chance to be on camera and describe the area you're traveling through.

Tour of the car. Since you're spending so much time in the car, why not feature the vehicle in a video segment.

Meet the crew. If your trip includes a plane ride, your children can describe each of the flight attendants and their jobs (before the plane moves and after landing).

Stocking up. Have your kids describe the special attractions of gas stations and rest stops.

To and Fro

By now your family video trip record is growing! (See page 188 for more video ideas while exploring your favorite vacation spots.)

What's Behind the Tray?

Kids love guessing games, especially if you can add a note of suspense by hiding the answer in an interesting spot. Your younger child will likely enjoy this airplane guessing game—it uses in-flight magazines to provide the mystery objects and the seat-back tray in front of you to conceal the answer until it's time to reveal it!

Required:
In-flight magazine/catalogue

Start by finding a picture in the magazine or catalogue that lends itself well to clues that your child will understand. A picture of a car, for example, can be hinted at by saying "We have one at home; it's something with wheels; it has four doors;" and so on. Fold the magazine so that your choice faces out (or tear out that page) put it on the tray, and fold the tray up to, as the flight attendant says, "its full upright and locked position."

After a predetermined amount of hints and guesses, or when your child gets the right answers, flip the catch, plop the tray down, and Taaa-Daaa—there's the answer!

To and Fro

What's in the Truck?

Required:
Writing supplies

What child isn't fascinated by the big trucks on the highway? Here's a simple way to parlay that interest into a fun activity that will help pass some time on the interstate.

First, have your children come up with a list of things trucks carry. The items on their list can be general or specific. The list could, for example, include "food" as well as "potato chips," or "construction materials" and "pipes."

As your children come up with items for the list, you or an older child can write them down, leaving room next to each entry to tally sightings. Then, have your children pick a time or distance at which to stop counting—say, 20 minutes or 25 miles (or, to add an element of the unknown, "at the third exit sign"). When everyone's ready, announce that you'll start counting in one minute (or one mile), and then see how many trucks your children can find that match their cargo list. They may also want to add new items to the list as they go along.

Let's see, that's three milk trucks, five moving vans, and one truck full of popcorn. Right?

To and Fro

What's My Job?

What does your child do for a living? Have him or her choose a job in the travel industry. Then family members can take turns asking questions such as the following:

- Do you wear a uniform? What does it look like?
- How long did it take you to get your license?
- How many miles do you log in one year?
- What's the most dangerous part of your job?
- What did you study to learn your job?
- What are your most important occupational skills?
- Can you take your family members with you when you work?
- What's the best part of your job?

The "worker" can give serious and helpful answers or silly ones. Either way, other players take turns guessing the occupation.

So, which answer made you realize that your child was a hot-air-balloon pilot?

To and Fro

Where on the Plane?

Required:

Writing and art supplies

For safety reasons, and to ensure the most comfortable flight possible, you and your family will want to locate key areas in the airplane, such as exits and bathrooms. Your kids can turn this into a game by drawing a diagram of the plane that shows where all of the crucial items are.

Take out a sheet of paper and have your child draw a diagram of the plane. If your child has been on a plane before or has seen pictures of the interior of an airplane, all the better; he or she can immediately incorporate some details—the cockpit, the doors, and so on—and then you can discuss what other things your child's drawing might include.

Once your child has finished his or her sketch and labeled as many items as possible, find the airplane safety-information card (which also contains a diagram of the plane's interior) in the seat-back pocket, and compare its picture with your child's version.

Now where did you say the bathroom was?

To and Fro

Who's on Board

With lots of stops and people getting on and off, determining who's on a train can be as interesting to your children as what's outside the window.

Have your children start a "Who's on Board" tally as soon as you're settled on the train. First, help them select a set of statistics to track. For example: how many people are in this train car; how many of them are girls, boys, women, men; how many people are traveling alone; how many people get on or off at each stop?

When your kids have their list of "demographic" questions, have them make a grid on a piece of paper to record the answers; it can show categories across the top and stops down the left margin. Then, have them tally and record the information at each stop the train makes. They can compare the different stops, noting which is the busiest, which is the quietest, and so on. For a variation, your kids can try to guess where certain people will get off the train. All aboard!

To and Fro

Who's Sitting Where?

Have your kids take a look around at their fellow passengers in the train car or compartment or airplane. Now have your kids close their eyes and ask them the following types of questions:

- How many people are in the car or compartment or plane (or the rows within the boundary set for this game)?
- How many of them are children?
- How many passengers are working or reading?
- How many people are wearing something blue?

Add your own people-related questions that are appropriate to your mode of travel. For example, if you're riding in an airplane and have to travel the aisle on the way to the bathroom, you might ask your child: How many people are sitting in the right side of the plane? How many people are watching the movie? How many passengers have their trays down?

Who knows? You might recall some of your fellow passengers as vividly as you do your vacation!

To and Fro

This game may be tame, but it's not the same as one that's lame. Your kids won't shun this fun in the sun or on the run. In fact, they may stop whining, drop what they're doing, and hop to attention.

To play, have your kids try to make a sentence using four words from a "word family" (a group of words that share beginnings or endings). For example:

- The mole in the hole stole a pole.
- The cat spat at the rat.
- The big rigs haul twigs and figs.
- The thin pin is in the bin.

Other word families your kids can use are those that end with *-an, -at, -it, -et, -ug, -en, -og, -op, -un, -ame, -ind, -ine,* and *-ing,* to name a few.

As your kids get good at making up these silly sentences, have them try for more than four words in each. And, of course, humor counts!

So, hug a bug and lug a rug; scan the plan to man the can; this quiz has a quiet quality that will quadruple your quotient of quick entertainment.

To and Fro

Word Games Galore

Required:

Homemade game board and cards (see activity 24), letter cards

Here are four word games you can do with a homemade game board (see activity 24). (Instead of affixing pictures to the cards, write letters on them.)

Hidden words. Place the letters in pockets to make words horizontally, vertically, and diagonally, then cover the letters with the other game cards. Take turns uncovering and recovering a single letter. When someone thinks he or she knows the location of an entire word, that person can uncover all of the letters in that word.

Rows and Columns. Randomly place letters on the board and take turns forming as many words as possible with the letters in a single row or column. Set a time limit or use the car's odometer.

Quick spell. Place all of the letters facedown on the board, then pick one at random for each child's turn. That player then has to find an object that begins with that letter and spell it.

To and Fro

Don't hesitate to make up your own word games, too. No one will get bored with this board!

Word Games on the Go

You can use the complimentary in-flight magazine on a plane or any other magazine to play a simple word-puzzle game with your older kids. Here's how. First, browse through the magazine and look for interesting pictures and phrases: pictures of animals, people, or cars; descriptive words used in advertising copy.

Required:
Magazines, writing supplies

Next, concoct a sentence in your head by combining the pictures and words. If, for example, you found a picture of a bear and one of a fish and the phrase "outrageously delicious," you might turn them into the sentence, "The bear ate the fish and said it was delicious."

Write down the sentence, leaving blanks for the pictures and words you found (in this case, bear, fish, and delicious). Below each blank, write a clue for the picture or phrase (for example, "a big, brown animal," "a great swimmer," and "tastes fabulous"). You can also include the page number.

Then hand the magazine and sentence puzzle to your children, and see how quickly they can fill in the blanks. Perhaps they will be inspired to make a puzzle for you!

To and Fro

Young Air Traffic Controllers

Required:
Cardboard tube, foil/magazine

Part of the thrill of an airport for kids—and many adults—is all the action as planes, cars, trucks, tankers, and luggage trains come and go. You can tell your child all about what the air traffic controllers do to make sure the vehicles don't get in each other's way, then visit observation deck of the control tower and let your child imagine he or she is in charge. (If the control tower doesn't allow visitors, find a window with a good view of the runway.) Then provide a pretend microphone. You can make one at home to bring along by adding a ball of aluminum foil to the end of a cardboard tube, or simply give your child a rolled-up magazine to talk into. Then he or she can begin directing planes to take off and land, carts to pick up luggage, trucks to deliver meals, and tankers to bring more fuel.

Of course, there are plenty of opportunities to add some zany fun. You can imagine the instructions your child may end up giving: "Okay, flight number six, you can take off now. Just watch out for the turtle and frogs on the runway!"

To and Fro

Your Great Photographer

There are bound to be some terrific photo opportunities during your travels, so why not designate your child as the unofficial family photographer?

Required:
Art supplies

Give him or her a small box, art supplies, index cards, or drawing paper cut into snapshot size pieces (8 1/2 x 11 paper cut into quarters). The box (which serves as a "camera") can have a viewing hole and a slot for the "undeveloped" snapshot paper, as well as a shutter button. Have your child look out the window and find something visually interesting to photograph. He or she can "shoot" the scene with their camera, remove the snapshot paper, and then "develop" the picture with crayons and markers (this is an "instant camera," after all).

When the picture is developed, the photographer can share the snapshots with his or her co-travelers (reminding people to hold the photos by the edges) so that everyone else can see what the photographer chose to capture on film. Perhaps the photo records something that only the photographer noticed, such as the taxi full of farm animals that was driving down the street!

To and Fro

III

There at Last!

161

First Impressions: The Environment

Required:

Family Book of Observations (see activity 31)

Even if you've traveled only a short distance, you're bound to notice some differences between your home and your surroundings when you reach your destination. Ask your kids the following kinds of questions as you tour the area.

- How far can you see?
- Is the land flat or hilly? Can you see mountains in the distance?
- What color is the soil?
- Is the air dryer or more humid than at home?
- Is the sky the same color?
- How do sunsets here compare with those at home?
- Does it rain more or less here than at home?
- Does it get dark earlier or later here than at home?

There at Last!

Your children can enter their findings in the Family Book of Observations (see activity 31) or, if they're pre-writers, report them to you or an older child with writing skills. Be sure to click a few pictures, too. Who, back home, would believe that you could see so far?

First Impressions: Houses

As you travel about town, have family members consider the architecture they see, noting, for the Family Book of Observations (activity 31), the differences and similarities to the architecture at home:

Required:
Family Book of Observations (see activity 31)

- What are the houses made out of— brick, wood, stone, adobe?
- Do they tend to be single- or multistory?
- Are there multi-family houses? Are the units side by side or one atop another?
- Are the roofs flat or peaked? If peaked, are they very steep or only slightly angled?
- What are the main colors of the houses?
- Do the houses have porches?
- Where are garages located?
- Are the yards big or small?
- What covers the ground in the front yards—grass, gravel, or plants?
- Where are the mailboxes?

When you get back, your kids will likely have a new awareness of your home and neighborhood, and a new understanding of the phrase, "There's no place like home."

There at Last!

First Impressions: Urban Architecture

Required:

Family Book of Observations (see activity 31)

Wherever you hail from, your family will no doubt find the downtown area of a new city or town interesting, especially when you compare it to home. Ask your kids questions like these, then log their answers in the Family Book of Observations (see activity 31).

- Are the downtown buildings taller than those at home?
- Are they old or new?
- What are the buildings made of—brick, limestone, glass?
- Do any of the buildings have gargoyles or other decorations?
- Is the city hall similar to the one back home? Would you have recognized it as the town's seat of government?
- Is the main library older or newer than the one in your city or town?
- What are the churches and other religious buildings made of, and are they similar to those where you're from?

How about this one: once you find the school, see if the playground structures are as much fun as those back home!

There at Last!

First Impressions: Streets and Sidewalks

Streets, sidewalks, trees, fences are some of the things that give each neighborhood its unique feel. As you and your family sightsee and shop, think about these kinds of questions:

Required:

Family Book of Observations (see activity 31)

- What are the streets and sidewalks made of—brick, asphalt, concrete, or cobblestone?
- Are the streets narrower or wider than those back home?
- Are there parking meters? Does parking time cost the same as back home?
- Where are the street signs—on the corner of a building, on a pole, or built into the curbs?
- What are the fences made of—wood or metal? Are they fancy or plain?
- Are there trees and flower boxes or flower pots along the sidewalks?

One thing is certain: after recording your answers in the Family Book of Observations (see activity 31), your kids will never take the sidewalks for granite again!

There at Last!

First Impressions: Flora and Fauna

165

Required:

Family Book of Observations (activity 31)

Travel is an ideal way for your junior naturalists to get a real appreciation for the diversity of plant and animal life. (Stress whatever "no touch" rules you have at home.) Here are some starter questions for your kids to answer in the Family Book of Observations (activity 31):

- Do you recognize any of the trees? Are the trees generally larger or smaller than those at home? Do most of the trees have broad leaves or needles?
- Are hedges common to the area? Do they look like the ones at home?
- Are there more or fewer flowering plants than at home? Do you recognize any of the wild flowers?
- What birds do you see? Do you recognize any of them from home?
- Are there any unusual insects?
- What small mammals do you see?
- Are there deer or other large mammals?

So your youngest child claims to have seen the Loch Ness monster by the sand dunes? Hope that you get all the details for the scientific community!

There at Last!

First Impressions: Everyday Life

Have your children take notice of everyday life in whatever city or town you're visiting; then record what they see in your Family Book of Observations (activity 31). There's sure to be some surprises!

Required:

Family Book of Observations (see activity 31)

- Do people generally seem more or less hurried than at home?
- How do shopkeepers and store clerks greet you?
- Do you hear any expressions that are new to you?
- Is the accent spoken here different from that at home?
- Do people dress the same here as at home? Are there any articles of clothing unique to the place or culture?
- Are hairstyles similar to or different from those at home? Do men have more or fewer beards and mustaches?

Now here's a real test of regional and cultural differences: Do the people here eat ice cream cones the same way as they do back home?

There at Last!

First Impressions: Food

Required:

Family Book of Observations (activity 31)

You have to travel pretty far from home before you can no longer find some semblance of a hamburger. But you'll encounter plenty of different foods or new ways of preparing familiar foods even if you're traveling only a few states away. Introduce your kids' palates to new and different foods wherever you're visiting, then record their findings in your Family Book of Observations (see activity 31):

- What do people eat for breakfast?
- Are there any unusual local specialties?
- What fresh fruits and vegetables are in season?
- How are potatoes or rice prepared?
- What is the bread like? Is it the same as at home?
- Do they have different names for foods or drinks than you do?
- Are certain spices commonly used?
- What are the favorite beverages?
- Do you find different condiments on restaurant tables here than at home?
- What do people eat for dessert?

There at Last!

So, how did you like the deep-fried alligator? Our kids tell us it's not nearly as tough as it sounds!

First Impressions: On the Go!

Municipal vehicles and public transportation—and cars, if you're traveling abroad—may look very different from the vehicles at home. Have your kids pay close attention to the various types of vehicles on the roads and streets, from two-wheelers to eighteen-wheelers. And pay attention to the roads and street themselves, too, as there are bound to be some interesting contrasts with home.

Required:

Family Book of Observations (activity 31)

- Are the cars large or small?
- Do drivers use their horns more or less?
- What color are the police cars?
- What color are the fire trucks?
- What color are the taxicabs? The buses?
- Are there subways or elevated cars? Monorails? Trolleys? Cable cars?
- Do people use bicycles for transportation? Mopeds?
- Are traffic lights suspended from wires or on poles?
- What color are the parking tickets?

Don't just *look* at the public vehicles. Why not take one to the museum or to lunch?

There at Last!

169 Camera Bugs

Required:
Single-use cameras

How many times do you wish you'd captured a particular moment on film—say, a spectacular sunset or a candid snapshot of family members doing endearing or zany things? You won't miss another photo if you have your junior photographers ready with their shutter buttons.

Outfit each of your family members with his or her own single-use box camera. This super-simple camera makes it possible for even three- and four-year-olds to take quality snapshots.

Next make a list of photo "assignments" that will give everyone a chance to chronicle the trip. One family member could be responsible for capturing sunsets and scenic vistas, while another does family portraits and group shots at historic sites. Another might be on "candid camera" detail.

You may also want to set up some guidelines about how many pictures are to be taken; this is a good opportunity for your kids to learn fiscal-photo responsibility and to really think about what they want to capture on film. Say cheese!

There at Last!

Chain Postcards

How well does your family function as a postcard-writing team? Here's a fun way to find out, while also generating some mail for the friends and relatives back home.

Buy a postcard during one of your travel stops or use one that your child makes from a blank postcard and art supplies. Choose a recipient by popular vote, or have each passenger take a turn picking a friend or relative.

The first traveler writes a sentence or phrase (pre-writers can dictate) and passes the postcard along to the next participant. This person adds a sentence or a phrase, gives it to another family member, and so on. The last person reads the postcard aloud. Once the message has been approved by all, stamp the postcard and begin a new one. (Make sure you designate someone to collect finished postcards and mail them.)

The message on the postcard can be serious or silly. What do you suppose the folks back home will say when they get a postcard saying, "Having a good . . . bright and sunny . . . wish you were . . . soon!"

Required:

Postcards, stamps, writing supplies

There at Last!

171 Sightseeing Tapes

Required:

Tape recorder

Are there any chatterboxes in your family? Here's a way to build on that strength.

To do this activity, you'll need a small tape recorder. Then, when you visit a museum, take a harbor cruise, hike through a forest, or stroll through a park, capture everyone's observations and experiences on tape. In an art museum, young children can describe which paintings have the most beautiful colors or the funniest people. Older kids might describe the historical period that the painting represents: what people wore, what they did for a living, the political structure, and so on. During a nature hike, everyone might comment on interesting plant life or birds. (See activity 165 for more observation suggestions.)

Family members can also interview each other, describing the "coolest" thing they saw, the most surprising, and what they'd recommend to their friends about the place.

There at Last!

When you play back the tapes a few months or a year later, you're bound to rekindle some great memories and a few belly laughs as well!

Hotel Counts

If your trip includes a stay at a hotel, here's something that turns exploring your surroundings into a fun activity. Set out with your kids in the spirit of exploration to find or count the following kinds of items. (Note: this activity is not intended to be done without supervision.)

Required:
Notebook, writing supplies

- everything that contains the hotel's logo, from to towels to insignias on uniforms
- the number of drinking fountains
- the number of pay telephones
- the number of ice machines
- the highest room number
- the number of Do Not Disturb signs on doorknobs
- the number of exit signs
- the combined cost of all items on the restaurant coffee-shop menu
- the number of plants in the lobby
- the number of hotel employees in the lobby at any one time

When you finish this activity, you might want to send the results to the corporate offices. They'd probably appreciate having a group of experts on tap!

There at Last!

Hotel Games

As exciting as hotels are for children, they can be a bit overwhelming at times. When your family arrives at a new hotel, take the time to explore it with your children, then try some of these quick activities when you're back in the room.

Map of the hotel. After your hotel exploration, have your children draw a map of the hotel, with the location of the elevators, swimming pool, front entrance, and so on. (This is also a good opportunity to point out to them where the emergency exits are located.)

Room-service fantasy. If your children could order anything at all from room service, what would it be?

Who works here? Have your children draw pictures of all the different people who work in the hotel—desk clerk, bellhop, concierge, valet—and discuss how these people make your stay nicer.

Who knows? By the time your kids get home, they may be ready for a career in hotel management!

There at Last!

Just Like Home

Here's a vacation pastime that will turn homesick blues (that can pop up even during the most exciting or interesting vacation) into a lively discussion and game.

As you and your family make your way through different places, have your children identify things in their new surroundings that are similar to things at home. They could, for example, find a house that's the same color or architectural style as yours, a street with the same name, familiar stores and businesses, a sign in a store window similar to one at home, a mailbox like yours, or a car or bicycle just like yours. You can have your kids simply announce what they see, or they can make a list to share with everyone else after a set amount of time.

See how many familiar items everyone can come up with, and perhaps take the opportunity to talk about how much you enjoy them at home.

Hey, there's somebody who looks just like Mrs. Jones!

There at Last!

175 Greetings from Afar

Required:
Postcards

Sending and receiving postcards is always fun, and the pictures are often a good addition to your own photos of special vacation spots.

You can have your child start his or her own collection of postcards by mailing them home from vacation. Then the cards will be waiting for your child when your family returns, ready to jump-start vacation reminiscing. Your child can write diarylike entries on the postcards, or pretend to be two different people, one sending the card and the other receiving it.

Encourage your child to include a lot of detail on his or her postcards, or to be as silly as possible. After all, he or she doesn't have to worry about confusing the recipient of the cards with comments about the giant squid that visited the harbor featured in the picture on the other side of the card.

If you're traveling with more than one child, you can have them send postcards to each other. But remember, no peeking! The cards can only be read back home.

There at Last!

Look Up!

The night sky at home may be a familiar sight, but how about the stars at your vacation destination?

If you've traveled some distance, see if anyone can pick out some "home" stars on a clear night. Are they in a different spot in the sky? What about the constellations? Are they positioned differently than they are at home? (You might want to make a trip to a bookstore before you go and purchase a star-gazing book.)

If you're visiting someone who lives out of the city and therefore away from reflections of buildings and car lights, your kids will probably be amazed at what they can see. Keep their eyes fixed on the heavens and see if anyone can find a shooting star.

You might also take advantage of a brilliant sky and ask your kids to invent a few constellations of their own. With so many stars to see, perhaps your kids will envision a celestial theater inhabited by such notable constellations as the Great Northern Chinchilla and Uncle Jack's Mustache!

There at Last!

177 Map Makers

Required:
Art supplies

This activity will give your kids an opportunity to exercise their cartographic skills and have some fun in the process.

Once your kids have gotten their bearings, ask each family member to draw his or her own map of the place you're visiting. The map should start with the place where you're staying, whether it's a hotel, motel, relative's house, or campsite. Then, based on your comings and goings, see if your kids can expand the map to include nearby roads, buildings, or landmarks that are of importance to them. When the maps are complete, study them to see what was considered worthy of representation.

The maps will serve as a fun record of what is of interest to your children. Should you return to the place, you can pull out the maps beforehand to rekindle fond memories. Be sure to have your kids revise the map when you revisit; the differences will help you chronicle your child's growth. Your kids will also get a chuckle when they see that they chose features such as the "really cool driveway" or the "neat climbing rocks."

There at Last!

Here's a neat way to get your kids focused on the interesting details at historical sites.

Stop at the information desk on your way in for a map as well as any brochures about special exhibits. Make up a list of things that can be found, then start a group scavenger hunt. You might also want to break up into teams led by an adult or older teenager. To get going, try finding these:

- an unusual architectural detail, such as an ornate drinking fountain, a decorative iron fence, or a stained-glass window
- old-fashioned clothing, cookware, drinking vessels, or musical instruments
- children's toys
- maps from the time period
- the best view of the site or surroundings (is there an observation point?)
- a painting of a child or family life
- things of interest that aren't on the map (exhibits in hallways, pathways, a sundial, a cannon)

How about this one: a hat as old as the one Dad wears while gardening?

There at Last!

Historic Site Queries

What would it be like to live history instead of just seeing it in a museum? The next time your family visits a museum, see whether you can find out.

Look through the museum for displays that might excite your children's imagination. Then ask them a series of questions related to what they are seeing. Frame the queries in terms of what your kids imagine life was like back then, especially for the children of the era.

For example, at an exhibition about the Middle Ages you might ask such questions as: What do you think children wore back then? Where do you think they slept? What foods do you think they ate? What kind of utensils do you think they used, and how are they different from the ones you use? What games do you suppose they played? What types of pets do you think the children had?

If there are guides stationed throughout the exhibition, assign an older child or an adult the task of asking them for the answers to your questions; then compare these answers to your children's.

There at Last!

There's more than one way to look at history!

Museum Copies

How many times, after a trip to an art museum, have you wished you could bring your favorite exhibits home with you? Here's one creative way to solve the problem: have your family make copies of the art.

Required:
Art supplies

First, you will need to provide each participant with his or her own sketch pad and colored markers or pencils. Then, as you work your way through the exhibits, choose some favorite paintings or sculptures. Remind your family artists that their drawings need not be accurate, but should instead try to capture the essence of what they are seeing, especially the features that attracted them the most to begin with. These might include the funniest, silliest, or scariest parts of the picture. Family members who prefer writing can describe the exhibits in terms of colors, shapes, lines, and so on.

Keep the drawings and written descriptions safe and clean during your trip through the museum (this can be the responsibility of an older child or an adult). Then, after you've arrived home, looking at them will be almost as good as taking another trip through the museum!

There at Last!

Museum Scavenger Hunt

Required:

Museum guides and maps, writing supplies

If you're looking for ways to make museum trips more exciting for your kids, give this activity a try.

First, stop by the information desk and pick up any maps and brochures about the exhibition. Before you set off on the tour, sit down for a moment, look over the materials, and devise a list of five to ten very specific things to hunt for. In a natural-history museum, these could include the T-rex skull, the Atlantic puffin, the trilobite diorama, gypsum needles, and the Audubon print of a giant egret; in an art museum, the list could include a painting of a vase of flowers and a pair of gloves on a table, a sculpture of a child with a bird, a mask from the Aleutian Eskimos, a small gold Mayan figure, a round fan, or "uchiwa," from Japan, and a sculpture of a ballerina with a real net skirt.

Once you've compiled your list, set off for the museum. You can either work together to find all of the items, or you can break into teams with specific assignments.

Perhaps you'll even find a painting of the man who looks like Uncle Fred!

There at Last!

Museum Find It

Here's a fun way to take a closer look at the exhibits in your favorite museum.

To begin, stop at the gift shop and purchase some postcards that feature pictures of exhibits (let everyone choose several). Then set out as a team to find each item featured in the postcards.

Required:

Postcards, museum map, writing supplies

If there are enough people in your group, you can form two teams. Give each team leader half the postcards; then each group sets off to find the appropriate exhibits. The group leaders can keep track of their finds, noting the precise locations on a map (you can usually get one at the information desk) or jotting down where the exhibits were found.

The teams reconvene at a preplanned time and place. Then the whole group takes another walk through the museum and plays a hot-and-cold find-it game. Each team tries to find the locations of the other team's postcards by following the other team's clues.

Who would have guessed that the sculpture of Venus would be located in the museum cafeteria?

There at Last!

Museum Memories

Required:

Paper,
pencil,
art supplies

After a morning spent at a museum, what did everyone learn? Here's a fun way to find out.

Soon after you've left a museum, or later that day, play a memory game with your family. Take turns describing in detail what you saw. What did you see first? Last? What was your favorite exhibit? The oldest? The biggest? The smallest? The most beautiful? The silliest? The scariest? This is also a perfect time to allow everyone to ask some questions. Did they understand everything they saw? Did it remind them of anything else?

Have a family member write down the answers. You may also want to ask everyone to make some drawings from memory to add to the reminiscences. This museum memory album may just turn into a permanent part of your family's collections.

The smallest thing? How about the ant crawling across the front steps as you went in!

There at Last!

Other Places Rated

Lots of books rate places according to economic indicators, housing, and so on. That's important stuff for grownups, but kids have other measures of what makes a town or city good to visit. With this activity, you can begin putting together your "Other Places Rated" book.

Required:

Notebook,
writing supplies

The day you leave a town or city, ask your kids to give you their opinions about how kid-friendly the place was, on a scale of one to three, based on:

- Were there many playgrounds or public parks?
- Were there special children's exhibits at museums?
- Were there enough ice-cream stores?
- Did the restaurants offer crayons and activity menus?
- Were there a lot of walls, rocks, or benches to climb on?
- Was there a good place to go swimming?
- Was it a good place to ride bikes?
- Was there a miniature golf course?

So, what do your kids think? Was your vacation choice a kid-friendly place?

There at Last!

Restaurant Reviewers

Required:

Notebook,
writing supplies

Luckily, restaurants are becoming more responsive to the needs of families; offerings such as kids' meals and booster chairs are more the rule than the exception these days. Here's a restaurant activity that will also tempt your kids to try new things.

First, equip your reviewers with a notebook set aside for restaurant ratings. You may want to choose a scribe, or you can take turns among older children. Then, after leaving each new restaurant, take a few minutes to write down your family's ratings.

Remind everyone that they are writing the review as if someone had asked his or her advice. Try to answer questions like: "What was the best item on the menu? What was best thing about the restaurant itself? What was the most unusual item offered?

Most important, did you get a balloon as you left?

There at Last!

Souvenir Scavengers

How would you like to go on the ultimate scavenger hunt and build a vacation memorabilia collection at the same time?

First, create a list of souvenirs—either found objects, freebies, or items purchased within a budget, for family members to find. The treasures should relate to your trip. For instance, if your family is vacationing in Washington, D.C., you might target "a picture of George Washington" or "something cherry-colored."

At the end of the day, see what each person found. A family scribe might be assigned to jot down notes about each object, and a "curator" should be designated to take charge of the whole collection until you return home.

What souvenirs do you suppose your family might uncover while walking along the reflecting pool of the Lincoln Memorial?

Required:
Writing supplies

There at Last!

Daily Vacation Journal

Required:

Looseleaf binder, writing supplies

A daily journal can be a great way to recall the day and preserve memories when you're visiting new places. All you need is a binder, paper, and pen.

Pick a time when everyone can contribute to the journal—perhaps during dinner or just before the children's bedtime. Each family member can make his or her own entry, or everybody can contribute to a group recounting of the day. One person can enter everyone's comments.

You can help your kids think of diary entries by asking them questions such as: What was your favorite excursion today? What's the neatest thing you learned? What was the funniest thing that happened? What did you do today that you would definitely want to do again next time we're here? Encourage your children to add drawings to their written entries, or tape in mementos such as ticket stubs and pictures from brochures.

There at Last!

Be sure to leave space for photos you'll be getting back when you return home (see activity 189). These will put the finishing touches on the perfect vacation diary.

Video Trip Record: There at Last!

If you've been videotaping your trip, you might want to add some unusual subjects in addition to your sightseeing and time spent relaxing around the pool. Here are some ideas on what to tape:

Required:
Video camera

Grand hotel. Enlist your child as an on-camera tour guide, pointing out highlights of the lobby.

Room with a view. Have your child describe the view from the windows of the room where your family is staying.

The shop on Main Street. If you spend any time in one place, your kids will have favorite shops and stops. Have them provide an on-camera commentary about what they like around town.

The not-so-incredible journey. Have your (supervised) older kids make a silly travel film of a trip to the ice machine, the bus ride to the museum, or walk to the spot where you parked the car.

Your children may find that the real --highlights of their trip turn out to be what they least expected!

There at Last!

IV

Home Again

Finishing-Touch Photos

Required:

Daily Vacation
Journal (see
activity 187),
self-adhesive
photo-
mounting
corners,
art supplies

Did you start a Daily Vacation Journal during your trip (activity 187)? If so, you can spice it up with photos that you and your children took during your travels. Here's how you can turn your picture-placing sessions into a celebration that the whole family can enjoy.

Select a time when everyone can sit down together to choose the best snapshots for your trip diary. You'll want to have a stock of self-adhesive photo-mounting corners and additional blank looseleaf pages.

Each family member should have the opportunity to select photos that complement his or her journal entries, and to write or dictate an appropriate caption. If you don't have a photo of a particularly interesting entry, your child can draw a picture. Also, have your children make a decorative cover to tape on the front of the binder and a title page that includes the places and dates of the vacation.

Find a place of honor for the journal in your family library. It may just become the favorite piece of literature on your shelf—not to mention a great resource for planning your next vacation!

Home Again

Vacation Newsletter

Want to tell the world about your most recent journey? Then publish your own "Just Back" newsletter.

Gather everyone together to pool their memories about the trip. If you kept a Daily Vacation Journal (activity 187), this is a good time to bring it out. Assign various subject areas to family members, such as "On the Road" or "In the Air" (describing your car trip or flight), "From the Navigator's Seat" (a description of the route), "Meals and Lodging" (interesting restaurants, local cuisine, hotels, motels, bed-and-breakfasts, campsites), "Great Sightseeing Spots" (museums, historic sites, and so on), and "The Family Funnies" (humorous incidents that took place during the trip). A younger child can dictate a story to you or an older sibling.

Once the stories are complete, number the pages, make a cover page containing the newsletter title and a table of contents, and take the entire issue to your local copy shop.

Pop the copies in the mail, and you might get a subscription request before you know it!

Required:
Art supplies

Home Again

Continuing Ed

Required:
Writing supplies, bowl, reference books

Your kids undoubtedly saw and absorbed a wealth of new ideas during your travels. Here's how you can extend the learning experience long after you've returned home.

First, create a list of topics to be researched based on your trip. For instance, if your family flew to your vacation destination, you might ask, "How does an airplane fly?" "How did airplanes of thirty years ago differ from the ones we fly in today?" Other questions might pertain to plants, architecture, or clothing that your children saw during your travels.

Write each question on a slip of paper and place it in a bowl. Then, have each family member draw a slip for a research assignment (people can trade or draw again if they'd prefer other topics). Your kids can use home reference sources or go to the library to prepare a five-minute report. The reports can be given during a dinnertime disscussion or a more formal evening presentation.

Who knows? Your family vacation might sow the seeds for a brilliant career in science, engineering, or anthropology for your child!

Home Again

Vacation Beat

Here's an unusual way to capture some favorite vacation experiences by turning your family members into household reporters.

First, with the help of your kids, create a list of interview questions. These might include the following: What did you enjoy most about your vacation? What was the funniest thing that happened on the trip? The biggest surprise? Who was the most interesting person you met? What was the most interesting sight you encountered? What single thing do you most want to remember about the trip?

Now have each family member take a turn interviewing the others. You can preserve the interviews if you have a tape recorder or video camera. Alternatively, you might have a family "journalist" turn the interviews into an article.

One way or another, your vacation is sure to make a worthwhile feature story!

Required:
Writing supplies, tape recorder/video camera

Home Again

193 Play It Again!

Required:
Writing supplies

Reminiscing about a family vacation can be a lot of fun. But you can take it further by re-creating a travel experience right in your own home.

First, gather together photographs, entries from your Daily Vacation Journal (activity 187), and any mementos you brought back from your adventures. Discuss which ones stand out as especially memorable. Perhaps there was a day spent watching dances and eating regional foods at an ethnic festival, an evening at a seaside restaurant after an afternoon on the beach, or a day strolling through a park near a relative's home. Make a list of ways you could re-create the experience by preparing a meal like the one you had there, finding and selecting music you heard, or re-enacting an event.

Assign each family member a job: helping prepare a grocery list or shopping, going to the library or music store to find a music tape or CD, helping to make a costume, and so on.

You may even want to invite some friends for a theme party. Who says your vacation has to come to an end?

Home Again

There's Always Next Time!

One of the hardest parts about leaving a favorite vacation spot is realizing you weren't able to "do it all." Here's a way to remind everyone that "there's always a next time."

Required:
Writing supplies

Once you're home, have a family gathering and assign someone the job of scribe. First make a list of all the things that your family did get to do on the vacation. Then make a list of the places that your family wasn't able to visit on this trip and activities you had hoped to do but just couldn't squeeze in. Encourage everyone to contribute an idea, whether it's a tour of a historic monument, a round at a miniature-golf course, a visit to an unusual store, or a ferry ride.

Be sure to have the scribe include enough information about each suggestion so that when it comes time to plan a similar trip, you'll have a good stock of ideas that you can be sure to place at the top of your list.

Perhaps you didn't tour the candy factory this time around, but next time, you and your kids will be sure to follow your noses to the home of the world's finest chocolate bars!

Home Again

Family Souvenir Gallery

Required:

Index cards, writing supplies

If your family tends to lose or forget the souvenirs they bring home soon after you unpack, here's an activity tailor-made for your household.

A few days after you return home, get everyone together to discuss how you can create a family gallery or exhibition hall to display all sorts of souvenirs and mementos. First solicit ideas for souvenir categories, such as "most unusual," "hardest to find," and "funniest." Make sure that everyone contributes at least one category or has items that fall under categories offered by other people. Next, make a list of the items that each person wants to contribute to the display.

A "curator" (you or an older child) then writes descriptions for each item on index cards, including the name of the item (for example, the "Great Alligator Tooth Rock"), where it was found, the date, and who found or purchased it.

Set up the exhibition again in a few months to remind people of the trip. Those seashells might be just the thing you need to chase away the cabin-fever blues on a snowbound day!

Home Again

Video Memories

A video camera is a great way to record impressions, thoughts, and feelings about your trip once you're back home. Try these starter ideas:

Required:
Video camera

Welcome home. Catch your children on video as they rediscover their house, pets, yard, and toys. Then play the tape back. Your kids may be surprised to see how happy they look to be back home again.

Interviews. Give each member of your family a chance to talk about his or her favorite parts of the trip. You can enlist your older children to conduct interviews and do the camera work.

Treasure hunters. Have your children describe the treasures they brought back with them.

Finally, be sure to have a family film festival a month or so after the vacation. Your children can wear their favorite souvenir T-shirts from the trip, and you can plan a dinner menu featuring foods from the places you visited. Then settle down, pop some popcorn, and roll the video for everyone to enjoy!

Home Again

Travel Reviewers

Required:
Writing supplies

If you relied on suggestions from friends or relatives to decide where to go on your trip, you know how valuable other people's travel suggestions can be. This activity gives your family members an opportunity to share your own recommendations with others.

A few days after you return home, call a family meeting, choose someone to act as scribe, then brainstorm a "review list" that includes items such as restaurants, hotels and motels, campsites, museums, historical sites, and the like.

Next, have everyone take turns dictating to the scribe his or her thoughts about each item on the review list, suggesting a rating from one to four stars. Compute the average for each review item to determine a final rating. Keep the results handy for friends and relatives.

Triple-A, look out. A new travel review machine is about to take over the marketplace!

Home Again

Alphabet Almanac

If you have early or pre-readers in your family, they'll enjoy making an alphabet almanac based on your travels.

Once you've unwound from the trip, supply your kids with postcards from your trip, pamphlets, and other printed materials that you don't mind discarding. Have your children begin by looking for pictures of things that begin with the letter *A* and cutting them out. Then glue or tape them in a notebook. Ask a child to draw a large *A* at the top of the first page, and continue the process through the alphabet.

Alternatively, glue the pictures to construction paper, punch holes, and bind the pages with yarn.

If a child can't find a picture corresponding to one or more letters, suggest that he or she draw something related to the vacation that contains the letter.

So, did you really see the *Q*ueen of Minnesota while you were staying at the Old O*x*en Hotel?

Required:

Travel literature, tape/glue, notebook/construction paper, hole punch, and yarn

Home Again

Friends from Afar

Required:

Loose-leaf notebook, ruled paper, alphabetical divider pages, writing supplies, self-adhesive photo-mounting corners, envelopes, stamps

One of the best parts of traveling is meeting new people and making new friends. To help you remember the friends your family made on the road, create an address book especially for keeping in touch with them.

You will need a small loose-leaf notebook, ruled paper, and alphabetical divider pages. A designated scribe can enter the names and addresses. If you took pictures of the people, affix copies to their pages in the address book using self-adhesive photo-mounting corners. Family members might also want to jot down interesting observations or facts about each person ("Joe has been making custom leather boots for 25 years, but he says each pair he makes is just as exciting as the first!").

Then send everyone in your book a copy of your Vacation Newsletter (activity 190) or any other memory preservers that you make. They'll no doubt be thrilled that you remembered them.

Home Again

Travel Show-and-Tell

With this family activity, you will be able to savor your best vacation times long after you've returned home.

Hold a show-and-tell session in which each family member discuss the following kinds of souvenirs:

Required:
Vacation souvenirs

- T-shirt with the name of a favorite city or town
- cap with a sports team based in a favorite city
- seashell or piece of driftwood from a beach
- rock or pine cone from a hiking trail
- postcard showing a sunset, scenic visita, or historic site
- piece of stationery from a hotel in a favorite town
- ticket from a museum, theme park, or theater

Each family member can give a two- or three-minute presentation. You might want to begin by having other family members guess why someone is so fond of a particular souvenir.

Okay, we give up. What's the significance of those acorns?

Home Again

Keeping in Touch

Just because the place you visited on your vacation is out of sight doesn't mean it also has to be out of mind! Have each person look out for news items related to the places you visited, such as:

Required:

Newspapers, scrapbook/box, tape/glue

Weather. Note temperature highs and lows from the weather map in your newspaper (*USA Today* and other major newspapers list temperature predictions each day for large cities).

Events. Clip articles from national newspapers in which the city is mentioned. Look for business news, presidential visits, and so on.

Local happenings. Ask friends or relatives who have access to the city's local newspaper to clip and send you any interesting news items relating to community events. Scan the articles specifically for mentions of people you met during the trip, places you visited, restaurants where you ate, stores you shopped at, and so on.

Home Again

Next time you plan a visit to this vacation spot, you'll surely be among the best-informed tourists!

Zany TV Travel Report

It's "Smith Trek," and the mission is to go where no family has ever gone before!

No, this isn't a new TV show—at least not in the conventional sense. The idea behind this activity is to have your children produce their own "television" show using a large box (you can often get one from an appliance store) from which you've cut out a screen and added a dial or two (yogurt-container tops affixed with brads). If you can't get a box, you can make a cardboard television facade with a large piece of posterboard.

Your kids can do on-location interviews, with the interviewee wearing beach clothes or a hat representative of one of the places you visited. He or she might also explain how certain foreign foods should be cooked or describe customs the family encountered in other parts of the world.

Or how about this one: your children can advise other kids on the best way to keep occupied while on the road. Take notes; you'll learn a lot for the next time you travel.

Required:

Large box/ posterboard, scissors/utility knife, yogurt-container tops, brads

Home Again

Resources

Miscellaneous Publications

- *Family Travel Times*, TWYCH (Travel With Your Children), 5 West 18th St., Seventh Floor, New York, NY 10011. $35 a year; includes access to back issues and opportunities to call in for specific information. An 8-to-12-page monthly newsletter that includes reviews (some written by kids) of resorts around the world, book reviews, and feature articles on travel. Special issues include an airline travel guide (great) and ratings of ski, cruise, and ranch vacations.
- "Kids and Teens in Flight" and "Fly Rights," U.S. Department of Transportation, Washington, D.C. 20036. Free. Call (202) 366-2220. Details special services for young travelers.

Books

- Dorothy Jordon and Marjorie Cohen, *Great Vacations with Your Kids* (New York: E. P. Dutton, 1992). Advice from the publisher of *Family Travel Times*, including details on city vacations and adventure vacations. Packed with good ideas on trip planning.
- Joanne Cleaver, *Doing Children's Museums* (Charlotte, Vt.: Williamson Publishing, 1992). A comprehensive guide book to 265 hands-on museums

across the country. Includes children's museums as well as science, natural history, and others, giving a good sense of each institution's strengths.

- Anthony D. Marshall, *Zoo: Profiles of 102 Zoos, Aquariums, and Wildlife Parks in the U.S.* (New York: Random House, 1994). Provides good information on each institution. Lots of details on the history of the zoo collections for anyone concerned about endangered species.
- Martha Shirk and Nancy Klepper, *Super Family Vacations: Resort and Adventure Guide* (New York: HarperPerennial, 1992). Rates upscale resorts, guest ranches, ski areas, historical places, and cruises. Organized geographically.

In addition . . .

Check out the "Traveling for Children" notes in all Fodor's guides and "Cool for Kids" in Frommers' guides for general family travel suggestions and things to do at specific destinations.

And when you get to wherever you're going, look for the local parenting publication for a detailed calendar of events and activities. They're available free in local libraries and stores in more than seventy cities across the country. For a complete list, contact Parenting Publications of America, 12715 Path Finder Lane, San Antonio, TX 78230-1532.

Please Share Your Travel Activities with Us

Do you have any favorite activities that your family enjoys when traveling by land, air, or sea (or variations of our activities)? We'd really like to hear about them. And if we use them in future editions of this book, we'll be sure to credit you by name. Send your ideas to:

Steve and Ruth Bennett
P.O. Box 382903
Cambridge, MA 02238-2903

(All entries become the sole property of Steve and Ruth Bennett.)

Index

Word, Math, and Map Activities

Great Exploration Activities

Road Games

Record Keeping, Trip Preservers